"Kris and his team of real estate rock stars are redefining the way real estate is sold right in front of our eyes. I'm telling everyone right now, 'You need to pay attention to this team and what Kris describes in this book!'"

—**CHRIS HAWKEY,** *The Power Trip* morning show host KFAN100.3; The Chris Hawkey Band

"I work with top real estate teams all around the country, and I can tell you what Kris Lindahl has created is genius—truly innovative. SOLD! *is an amazing book that will teach homeowners to step up and realize there is a better method out there.*"

—**DARIN DAWSON,** founder of BombBomb.com

"This easy read is jammed-pack full of great information when it comes to the steps necessary to selling your home. Kris has an innovative approach that is getting national recognition and, more importantly, benefiting every seller his team works with."

—**JOHN COLLOPY,** founder & CEO, RE/MAX Results

"We have bought and sold six houses with Kris Lindahl and his team. The most recent one sold $36,000 over listing price in less than a week! The forward-thinking strategies they teach in this book are the exact same ones that they used to sell our house. The process is genius when it comes to preparing your home for sale, marketing, and attracting offers. We were blown away when we found out we had several offers over asking price. If you are thinking about selling your home, the only one to call is The Kris Lindahl Team."

—**KIM & TROY COULSON**

W9-AZK-872

FOREWORD BY **DAVE L. LINIGER**, CEO OF RE/MAX

EXPERT ADVICE ON

HOW TO POCKET

MORE MONEY ON

YOUR HOME SALE

KRIS LINDAHL

CONTRIBUTING AUTHOR:
SARAH PICKENS

Advantage®

Published by Advantage, Charleston, South Carolina.
Member of Advantage Media Group.

ADVANTAGE is a registered trademark, and the Advantage colophon is a trademark of Advantage Media Group, Inc.

Printed in the United States of America.

ISBN: 978-1-59932-809-6
LCCN: 2016963409

Cover design by Megan Elger.

This publication is designed to provide accurate and authoritative information in regard to the subject matter covered. It is sold with the understanding that the publisher is not engaged in rendering legal, accounting, or other professional services. If legal advice or other expert assistance is required, the services of a competent professional person should be sought.

Advantage Media Group is proud to be a part of the Tree Neutral® program. Tree Neutral offsets the number of trees consumed in the production and printing of this book by taking proactive steps such as planting trees in direct proportion to the number of trees used to print books. To learn more about Tree Neutral, please visit **www.treeneutral.com.**

Advantage Media Group is a publisher of business, self-improvement, and professional development books. We help entrepreneurs, business leaders, and professionals share their Stories, Passion, and Knowledge to help others Learn & Grow. Do you have a manuscript or book idea that you would like us to consider for publishing? Please visit **advantagefamily.com** or call **1.866.775.1696.**

To my daughter, Victoria.

V, You are my reason! I couldn't have asked for a more amazing daughter. You are beautiful both inside and out. I am honored to be your father, and I can't wait to watch you grow into the incredible woman I know you will become. Your smile melts my heart, your laughter brings me joy, and your love is my everything. You will always be my rock star!

—Daddy

TABLE OF CONTENTS

LEGAL DISCLOSURE

The information presented herein represents the view of the author as of the date of publication. This book is presented for informational purposes only. While every attempt has been made to verify the information in this book, neither the author nor his broker assumes any responsibility for errors, inaccuracies, or omissions.

Any reference to websites, vendors, products, and services does not represent an endorsement by the author.

This publication comes with the understanding that neither the author nor the broker is engaged in rendering legal, accounting, financial, or other professional service. If legal advice or other expert assistance is required, the services of a competent professional person should be sought.

Kris Lindahl is a licensed real estate broker in the State of Minnesota and a licensed salesperson in the State of Wisconsin. Kris holds his license with RE/MAX Results.

If your home is listed with another real estate broker, this book is not intended to be a solicitation.

FOREWORD

When I was a teenager in the farmlands of Indiana years ago, I started reading the books that would change my life. I had big dreams, and I devoured the ideas of great business leaders and thinkers. Reading consumed me and put me on a course of lifelong learning and personal development.

Nothing has changed in that regard. I read whenever I can, listen to audiobooks in the car and on flights, and enjoy learning new things at every opportunity.

Reading *SOLD!* is a real treat because the insights it contains are right up my alley. It's rewarding to see what a real estate maverick like Kris Lindahl is doing to shake things up and go above and beyond for his clients.

In the forty-four years since I founded RE/MAX and began building the world's premier global real estate brand, I've come to notice common elements in the dynamic agents who excel at serving their clients and staying ahead of the pack: relentlessness; innovation; creativity; work ethic; fine-tuned systems; collaboration; confidence; and, especially, an unending passion for solutions that question the norm, crush the competition, advance the industry, and create the best possible outcomes for clients.

That passion and those qualities come through loud and clear in *SOLD!* Kris Lindahl is a rising star who understands the winning combination for successful entrepreneurs of any era—that you can't do today's business with yesterday's methods and expect to be in business tomorrow.

As he illustrates so well in *SOLD!*, selecting the right agent—and often the right team—is a key decision for anyone buying or selling a home. There are often big differences among the options, and choosing someone with skills, systems, and a proven track record is usually the best way to go.

Early on in *SOLD!* it's clear that Kris is an innovator and disruptor at heart, never content to do things "the way they've always been done." Instead, he questions the status quo and gladly makes his competitors uncomfortable. Consider this excerpt: "Realtors have sold homes in more or less the same way for many decades. Tradition and inertia might make it appear normal—it's how you sold your last house and how your parents sold theirs—but in fact this strategy, or lack of strategy, is completely archaic and broken."

That's the voice of someone pushing hard to improve the process for buyers and sellers—someone committed to finding a better way.

Of course, it's one thing to say, "the traditional approach doesn't work anymore," and quite another to say, "the traditional approach doesn't work anymore, and here's how I've reinvented it to better serve my clients." That's the real magic in *SOLD!* Kris doesn't just criticize the norm; he enhances it. For instance, his team doesn't market a home to a series of individual, semi-interested prospects. Instead, they systematically reach every potential buyer in the area, creating a competitive environment where the house is the grand prize everyone wants. That's a win for any seller. With his full-market strategy—a truly game-changing concept—Kris turns the process on its head, creating excitement, urgency, and action. That's not just a *different* approach; it's a *better* approach.

Another example is the makeup of the Kris Lindahl Team itself. Kris hasn't assembled a collection of similar agents. He's built a strategic operation in which every individual contributes specific, unique abilities and skills. His world-class specialists work with a shared vision, providing clients with the best in staging, photography, digital promotions, and expert follow-up services. The result is a far richer experience for clients and a far greater impact.

Whether their aim is to maximize portal exposure, drive traffic to a property website, use feedback data to make highly informed decisions, help sellers renovate for higher returns, or market like the digital ninjas they are, Kris and his team do all they do with one goal in mind: providing irreplaceable value to the clients.

With laser-like precision, Kris and his team close hundreds of sales a year, helping hundreds of families achieve their real estate goals. That's a huge number, and it can only be reached through skill, professionalism, and quality. These things matter . . . a lot.

I've seen virtually everything at this point, but I've never stopped learning. I'm smart enough to know that I don't know it all. But as much as the world has changed through the years, the essence of what makes some agents stand out remains the same. Excellence belongs to people willing to reject the easy route, find the better way, and achieve their goals by helping others achieve theirs.

People like Kris Lindahl.

Kris has what I call "a fire in the belly"—a relentless drive to be extraordinary. That fire is apparent on nearly every page of his incredible book. People with fire in their bellies lift everyone around them, and Kris is no exception. His insights will help buyers and sellers be smarter about what they're trying to achieve and help other real estate agents be more open to fresh ideas and new, better methods.

So, enjoy reading *SOLD!* And keep your copy handy. I'm sure you'll revisit it from time to time.

DAVE LINIGER

CEO, Chairman, and Cofounder
RE/MAX, LLC

INTRODUCTION

NEW WAYS TO GET THE MOST FOR YOUR HOME

ost people don't have to look far in their social circles to find real estate agents. Whether they're neighbors from down the block, friends of friends, relatives, or the same firm of Realtors®[1] family members have used for generations, real estate agents are a dime a dozen.

Homeowners often hire an agent simply because he or she is a friend or neighbor or has been recommended by a single source, but how many of these traditional real estate agents can maximize the return on what's probably your biggest asset, your home? Most sellers can't answer that question because they don't research the agents they hire. Many don't think such research is necessary and others, who would like to dig deeper, don't know where to begin. This scenario needs to change—and quickly!

I decided to write this book after years of watching homeowners lose thousands and thousands of dollars on the sales of their homes,

---

[1]   The capitalized word *Realtor*® specifically refers to a real estate agent who is a member of the National Association of Realtors®.

using the outdated sales process traditional real estate agents rely on. The business has changed significantly, but many agents have been slow to catch up with the massive shifts in technology, marketing, and sales adopted by other industries.

The prevailing mind-set among consumers is that all real estate agents and brokers are created equal. This couldn't be further from the truth. My mission in these pages is to explain the many ways that the traditional sales process is broken and to highlight its very concrete costs to sellers. I want to educate you about other options and provide the tools to help you choose a new kind of real estate professional, a dynamic agent who can sell your home quickly, for top dollar.

I want to educate sellers, but this book is not theoretical or abstract. It's brimming with real-life examples and firsthand experiences from my own extensive real estate career. I have had the distinct privilege of working with thousands of buyers and sellers, so as you can imagine, I have dealt with virtually every possible situation. This vast expanse of transactions gave me the experience and insight I needed to re-invent the traditional selling process that Realtors® have used for generations: stick a sign in the yard, put the listing in the MLS, and wait for another agent to bring a buyer.

Sorry, that just doesn't cut it anymore!

My team and I have replaced this broken old-school approach with dynamic techniques that bring the entire market to your home. We have leveraged the latest strategies in marketing and technology for a sales approach that has more in common with companies like Apple and Tesla than with traditional brokerages. The dynamic agents on our team use these cutting-edge techniques with every home we list, and their success has been proven again and again.

You can't afford to be in the dark when it comes to your real estate agent and the process he or she uses to market the biggest investment of your life. You can't afford a traditional approach that's decades out of date when a more dynamic strategy that can maximize your sales price exists.

I am passionate about everything I do, and giving others the tools to succeed has always been a top priority for me. From a young age, I wanted to be a leader who educated others. That desire motivated me to earn a degree in education from Minnesota State University, Mankato and later to create a team of real estate rock stars with more than a hundred years of combined industry experience.

Before people can educate others, they have to learn, and I spent many years in the trenches, finding the flaws in an outdated system and crafting solid solutions. I tried many methods and techniques over the years—some successful, others not—and spent lots of dollars finding ways to put more money in the pockets of my sellers. Not all my ideas worked, but a diligent student in the school of experience, I persevered, became an industry leader, and through trial and error, developed the successful techniques I use for sellers and buyers today.

What do I mean by successful? When you sell a home using the exclusive marketing plan I designed for my team, you get a "full-market response." I'll explain this term in great detail throughout the book, but it essentially involves a strategy that brings the entire market to your home in a competitive environment in order to maximize sales price and minimize market time.

Don't take my word for it. Using this innovative system, my current real estate team became one of the top ten in the country in less than two years. As I wrote this, our innovation and expertise had us on track to sell more than seven hundred homes in 2016. The Kris Lindahl Team has been an industry leader year after year in the

Twin Cities metro area. (You can learn more about our approach and services at www.KrisLindahl.com.)

The lessons I've learned developing my business aren't taught in the classrooms, where people spend shockingly little time before they get their real estate licenses. Poor education is a problem throughout the real estate industry, one I have taken on as a daily challenge, working to change the way homes are bought and sold. I educate my buyers and sellers about a better process, and now, I want to educate you.

In the following chapters, I'll explain the pitfalls that so often result in poor service, ineffective marketing, long market times, and lower home prices. I'll explain a better approach, explode the myths, and give you concrete questions to ask agents to ensure that you're hiring a dynamic, forward-looking professional. This checklist alone could save you many thousands of dollars at closing time.

Thank you for taking the time to read this and learn about a better, proven real estate sales process. I want to improve the entire real estate industry one sale at a time, but meanwhile, I take great satisfaction from helping you improve your bottom line, lower your market time, and say "SOLD!" with a smile.

CHAPTER 1

LIST AND PRAY: HOW *NOT* TO SELL YOUR HOME

Remember the last time that you or someone you know sold a home? Here's how the process probably went.

You hired a real estate agent based on a referral. Your cousin or coworker or former neighbors had used a particular agent—John Smith, say—and liked him pretty well. But is liking someone sufficient logic to trust them with one of the biggest financial investments in your life?

John came out to see your house, and he was a nice guy, professional and experienced. He'd been selling real estate for more than fifteen years and had deep roots in the community, which he demonstrated. He knew the local school districts, the parks, the restaurants. John knew the neighborhood so well, he promised that he could price your home expertly. He promised to get the most the market would bear in the shortest possible time, and of course, you liked the sound of that.

John printed listing sheets for several comparable properties, then determined what he wanted to sell the place for. He asked you to tidy the house up for tomorrow, when photographs would be taken.

The next day, John's assistant, or possibly John himself, showed up to snap some pics on a digital camera or cell phone.

In the front yard, John stuck a big sign, bearing his name and number. He entered the house in the local multiple listing service (MLS), the system real estate agents have long used to exchange information about properties, and he put it up on his company's corporate website. He held a couple of "open houses" early on, and for these, he stuck an extra sign with an arrow on the street corner to catch stray passersby who might be interested. Some attendees at these open houses turned out to be looking for very different types of properties, and some were just nosy neighbors and real estate buffs, but a couple showed genuine interest.

Within a week, John started scheduling individual appointments, too, one for Monday morning at ten o'clock, a Wednesday at two o'clock in the afternoon, and then one for the next Sunday at dinnertime (for a buyer with a busy schedule). The appointments were awkward, especially that Sunday one, as strangers breezed through your home at all hours on random days, but this, you understood, was how people sold houses. At least John was doing a good job.

The house didn't sell in the first week or two, as you'd fantasized—maybe not even in the first five or six weeks—but being the pro that he was, John recommended adjustments along the way to help. The couple with the Thursday noon appointment noted how dark the dining room seemed, and John thought there might be something to that. He recommended painting it a lighter, more neutral color, and antsy to sell, you agreed. A fellow viewing the house the following week thought it was priced too high, by perhaps $20,000. After watching your home sit on market for six weeks and noting fewer appointments lately, John took such feedback seriously.

He suggested reducing the price by $15,000, and reluctantly, you agreed.

Maybe listening to that feedback paid off. Less than a week after the price reduction, you found yourself accepting an offer. Another real estate agent had seen John's listing in the MLS and brought over a client who liked your house and location. The offer was for less than you'd hoped, but as John pointed out, it was for all that the market would bear. And because this was the only process you knew of, it was enough. But now there are other options—options that can make you more money.

A BROKEN PROCESS

If this process sounds familiar, that's because Realtors® have sold homes in more or less the same way for many decades. Tradition and inertia might make it appear normal—it's how you sold your last house and how your parents sold theirs—but in fact, this strategy, or lack of strategy, is completely archaic and broken.

Step back and take an objective look at the process. For starters, it is disruptive for sellers, who must cater to buyers showing up randomly at all hours. What passes for "market feedback" (leading to costly price changes and home improvements) is merely the slow trickle of those buyers' whims, collected haphazardly at individual appointments. They don't reflect the overall market in any way; rather, they merely represent the take of a few random shoppers. John's "list-and-pray" approach, as I call it, offers all the marketing savvy of your eleven-year-old's lemonade stand. A yard sign is the centerpiece of both efforts—yet your *Realtor's®* costs tens of thousands of dollars in commissions.

The bottom line is that John's old-school approach is not helping your bottom line. Traditional Realtors® promise to get the most that the market will bear for your home in the shortest possible time—and that's laudable. Too often, though, their actions are completely incongruous with that goal.

To get the most the market will bear as quickly as possible, sellers need an agent—in fact, a team—that can get the *full market* to participate in the sales process. The goal for John and other traditional agents is to find *a buyer*. There's the first problem. The goal of a *dynamic agent* should be to find *every buyer* in the marketplace who could potentially purchase a home and then to systematically place them in a competitive environment, with the home as the prize. In this model, efficient full-market participation replaces an overreliance on individual appointments and reduces market time. Full-market feedback replaces the slow trickle of random buyers' opinions. Sophisticated, targeted marketing replaces the old list-and-pray method, and sellers see results that justify their costs.

The 6–7 percent in agent commissions (split between the agents of both the buyer and seller) paid on a house that sells for, say, $600,000 is $36,000. That's an awful lot of money to pay someone to stick a sign in a lawn, dump a listing in the MLS, and have Bob from the office snap a few pics. Incredibly, though, this remains a pretty good description of the typical sales effort in residential real estate. Oh, sure, your house will also appear on a giant corporate website that's the equivalent of a black hole in cyberspace, but the fundamental approach hasn't changed since the 1960s.

Considering the revolutions we've seen in technology and communications during the last couple of decades, what industry besides residential real estate has maintained the same sales and marketing strategies?

Think of companies like Netflix and Amazon. Movies are now sold and rented in completely new ways. The corner video store became a dinosaur as consumers took to "streaming" films online and storing them in the "cloud," euphemisms that roll off the tongue now but didn't exist not so long ago. Interested in a show? At Netflix, you can see with one click what the entire viewing market thinks of it, with hundreds of reviews and aggregate ratings. In Amazon, booksellers now have a funnel that targets the entire market for a particular product and brings it to them. The days of placing books on shelves and hoping they stand out for buyers trickling through have disappeared (and so, to a large extent, have bookstores).

Real estate, though, is marketed and sold almost exactly as it was half a century ago. Already, I can hear some readers protesting, what about Zillow and Trulia and other real estate websites? Sure, those sites are innovative and have some admirable features. Buyers are using them to browse and gather information, searching for homes in new ways, especially early in the process, but what has changed for *sellers*?

Whatever websites a traditional agent uses, the process is more or less the same. A second-rate photo appears on Zillow with the agent's number. A tiny percentage of the potential buyers who could be interested in this home bother to click on it and call the agent, who sets up individual appointments. A buyer comes to see the home, which hasn't been properly prepared for sale, and gives random feedback, which gets relayed to the sellers haphazardly. If the sellers are lucky, an offer comes in. Is it the highest price the market can bear? Maybe. Maybe not. The seller hasn't gotten anything close to full-market participation, so there's no way of knowing what the actual fair-market price might have been. Zillow is a tool like any other—a spiffy tool with potential—but in the hands of traditional agents without a proven process behind them, it's essentially a virtual yard sign.

POOR EDUCATION, EASY LICENSING

Look, I don't want to be too hard on John Smith, the traditional agent in our example. John—and his sister Jane—are nice people, and they're not trying to rip you off or avoid extra work. They're doing things the only way they know how, just as they were taught, which is to say, inadequately. Real estate sales strategies generally lag behind those of other industries because we have a poor education program for Realtors® and minimal licensing requirements. Real estate school is quick and simple. Realtors® teach students how to pass a test—not how to sell homes—and then they're handed licenses. They go to work at a traditional office where a broker who was an unsuccessful agent in his or her day trains them in the same shoddy methods that got him mediocre results.

If John Smith earns $40,000 as an agent, he'll be doing well, and if Jane cracks $50,000, she'll earn more than most. Whether a Realtor® is in San Diego or the Twin Cities, he or she will be lucky to see four closings this year (the average per agent in both places is fewer than four per year). Think about this. Sellers trust an asset worth hundreds of thousands of

THE SELLER PAYS TENS OF THOUSANDS OF DOLLARS TO SOMEONE WHO IS UNSUCCESSFUL 360 DAYS A YEAR.

dollars, if not millions, to a poorly trained person using outdated methods that garner success perhaps half a dozen times in a good year. The seller pays tens of thousands of dollars to someone who is unsuccessful 360 days a year.

Sellers might think they'll get great service as one of only three or four clients their agent will close that year, but consider the resources available to someone earning $40,000. Is he or she plowing any of that money back into marketing efforts to promote the business and sell listings, to build and maintain a top-notch website, to harvest data and create targeted buyer lists, to produce stunning photos and brochures, to hire the kind of team needed for a full-market response? Not if he or she also wants to eat and keep gas in the car.

LOSING ONE BUYER AT A TIME

I've mentioned several influential companies that have changed how we sell and buy, but the sad truth is, we don't need to look to market leaders to see how antiquated real estate sales efforts are. Car dealerships aren't exactly cutting edge, but they're far more efficient than most real estate brokerages. The car dealer does not empty out the lot to shepherd individual buyers through the showroom. It's a ridiculous image, sure, but this is essentially what real estate agents who rely primarily on individual appointments do. Does Apple want to pitch its latest iPhone to customers one at a time? Is that how Amazon sells all manner of products online? Of course not. What industry besides real estate operates in this way?

I've already highlighted the maddening inconvenience of an overreliance on private showings for sellers, but that's not the worst of it. Most sellers would suffer through week after week of individual appointments if it meant they were getting the best price the market could bear for their homes. In fact, an overreliance on individual appointments does the opposite. It forces each buyer into an environment that puts him or her in direct competition with the seller. No other buyers are present in the house, and there's no sense of competition, so naturally, the potential buyer focuses on the seller. "How do I get the best price?" the buyer thinks. "How low will the seller go?"

Individual appointments have their place, but they should be supplemental and used strategically *after* we have created a competitive environment that pits buyers against buyers. Otherwise, the appointment simply pits buyer versus seller. What a terrible model! Consider this situation: When you walk into a car dealership and you are the only one looking at a car, you begin to question how low you can negotiate. However, if there are multiple buyers all eyeing the same car as you, it creates a sense of demand and urgency—and you are likely thinking, *What is the highest I am willing to pay for this car?* because you don't want to lose to the competition.

The reality is that most businesses don't rely primarily on individual appointments because this approach is not only uncompetitive, but it also leaves the seller without true feedback. If a single customer at a car dealership passed up the opportunity to purchase his dream car because it was out of his price range, this would likely not worry the salesman. But if the next twenty visitors to the lot expressed the same sentiment and complained of the unrealistic price of the car, well, it might be time to charge less.

Companies like Apple make it a priority to create urgency and move products. Apple wants everyone to see that line down the block as shoppers camp out for its latest iPhone. The line ignites a sense of competition in potential customers. A store that's empty, save for one customer, does the opposite, dooming a sales effort. Product that sits grows stale for buyers, and this basic psychological response applies to homes, too. Home sellers waiting for trickle-in feedback from individual appointments see their homes stagnate on the market for thirty, sixty, ninety days before they make adjustments (based on random opinions). By then, their position has weakened. Every day that your home sits on the market erodes your power as a seller, depleting buyers' interest and urgency—and making them wonder why your place hasn't moved.

Of course, John or Jane Smith also held some "open houses" when she put your hypothetical home on the market. Multiple buyers showed up to these events, right? No. Not many, and certainly not the right ones. Sticking a sign on the corner and hoping that people on their way to buy ice cream might see it—and also be in the market for just this kind of property—is not very effective. Sticking an "open house Sunday" banner on a scattershot newspaper ad is also a fairly blunt attempt to reach the target market. Actually, it's not quite fair to say that traditional open houses miss the target market. Agents who use this cornerstone of the list-and-pray approach never figure out what the target is, and *if they don't know what they're aiming for, how can they be said to miss it?*

A FULL-MARKET RESPONSE

What is the alternative to this broken, antiquated sales approach and to traditional real estate agents like John and Jane Smith? I'll present the answer step by step in the following chapters, demonstrating how today's dynamic agent can generate the full-market response, true feedback, and sophisticated marketing needed to get the highest price the market will bear for your home in the shortest possible time.

Traditionally, real estate agents have sold their access and knowledge. Sellers paid for Realtors'® access to the MLS. How else would homeowners see the "comparable sales" that allowed them to price their property? How else would they expose it to local Realtors®? Agents sold their knowledge of the local market and of the community, too—their takes on the schools, parks, restaurants, shops, etc.

Most agents, sadly, are still touting such access and knowledge at a time when technology has made them obsolete. Anyone with a laptop or phone can find much richer information about school districts, restaurants, and parks than any agent can supply. While sites like Zillow and Trulia often contain errors, they also have value, and the Internet generally has made pricing and sales data much more accessible. The MLS is an important tool, but if you're paying a Realtor® for access to it, you'd be better off attempting to sell your own home.

To justify the hard-earned money you're paying them, dynamic sales agents should outline a proven process that gets a full-market response. They should back up the promise to get the highest price the market will bear for your home, in the shortest possible time, with concrete steps. The old "list-and-pray" approach just doesn't cut it anymore.

In the chapters ahead, I will discuss proven strategies that bring the full market to a seller's home *at one time*, instead of bringing buyers there one at a time. Individual appointments have their place, but in my dynamic approach, they are strategic, supplementary, and subordinate to the creation of a highly competitive environment. No more endless appointments, and no more trickle-in feedback. Instead, I'll outline a process that creates urgency and stokes competition. I'll explain how I leverage the agent population and create proprietary lists to target the most likely buyers. As part of a successful strategy, pricing should be based on broad market participation in a thorough valuation, not one person's opinion, and this, too, must be built into the process.

Marketing is key to a successful sales effort, but technological advances have hurt, not helped, the Smiths' efforts, highlighting the shortcomings of an outdated approach. It's easier than ever to snap and manage amateur photos, which leads traditional agents to think that their photography skills, or their assistants', are good enough. In fact, buyers browsing real estate websites will only stay on a listing photo for a second before moving on. John's second-rate pics might have squeaked by when black-and-white newspaper ads ruled the day, but they are so many nails in the coffin of a contemporary sale. The same holds true for the shabby "brochures" he can now easily and cheaply print out at the office and the free cookie-cutter company website where he can dump listings.

An effective marketing strategy and a full-market response require a level of sophistication and resources that traditional agents can't access. They should not only be hiring a professional architectural photographer to win with presentation, but they also need a web developer to create a site that's unique and functional. They should have a stager to prepare the house, a listing manager to handle traffic, a contract-to-close specialist to handle paperwork, an administrative assistant to provide office support, among other team members.

Dynamic agents (like my team and I) understand that achieving a full-market response is a complex process that requires an entire team of professionals. The team effort is so important that I'll devote the next chapter to explaining how my team works and analyzing the benefits of having a team, rather than a single agent, sell your home.

CHAPTER 2

DYNAMIC AGENTS: IT TAKES A TEAM

When I sell a home, I use a proven process that's very different from the one used by John or Jane Smith, the traditional Realtors® from our example in chapter 1. I'm not concerned about catering to a buyer at ten o'clock in the morning on Tuesday and a buyer next Friday at three. As a dynamic agent, I aim for *all buyers* in the marketplace who could potentially purchase a particular home. I target them precisely, reach them efficiently, and funnel them all into a competitive, expertly managed environment.

My process, which gives sellers true feedback and a full-market response, is much more complex than John or Jane's. They couldn't pursue this strategy even if they knew how, because it requires a team of specialists. With four closings and an income of perhaps $40,000 per year, John is lucky if he can afford a part-time assistant, much less the services of an entire team of experts.

The one-person "list-and-pray" approach is familiar to anyone who has ever sold a home, but parts of a more modern and dynamic strategy probably won't be. In this chapter, I'll walk you through my process and highlight the roles of the various team members who make it possible. My strategy cuts down on hassles and worries for sellers, and much of what I'll describe happens quietly, behind the scenes. Homeowners don't need to keep up with the activities of various team members—or even know that some of them exist— while they're selling any more than drivers need to understand the suspension and steering systems on their new car while driving. I provide a brief overview here simply so that sellers can have confidence in what's under the hood with the team approach and appreciate why it makes for a smoother, faster, and more efficient ride.

When homeowners call John or Jane Smith to inquire about selling a home, the odds are good that they'll get voicemail, and when the call will be returned—Wednesday, Friday, next week—is anyone's guess. This is because John and Jane work alone and take all of their own calls. If they're lucky, they might share an administrative assistant with other agents, but this unlicensed, minimally trained person can't do much more than deliver messages.

The team-based approach, by contrast, begins with a professional who is always ready to field that first inquiry from a seller. The dynamic agent has professionals on-hand who are ready to talk to sellers all day. Rather than getting voicemail, my sellers immediately talk to a live person who has been trained to discuss their property needs. Remember, if an agent fields all his own calls and can't take yours, *buyers* calling him about your house later will get the same treatment. Personally handling all client calls means missing client opportunities.

After the *intake specialist* has recorded basic info about a home, such as the address, number of bedrooms and bathrooms, the square footage, and key features, he or she sets a time with the sellers when a *listing specialist* can come out to assess the home and meet the homeowners. This vital team member, as the title implies, is focused entirely on servicing sellers and shepherding their listings to the point of sale. This is the listing specialist's only job, morning, noon, and night.

The listing specialist will meet with the sellers, assess the property, and discuss pricing. Because this expert is a licensed real estate agent focused on listings all day every day, he or she can help sellers quickly and accurately price their home based on its condition and features, using his or her analysis of recent sales of comparable properties nearby as a guide. This initial step usually happens in one or two visits. The listing specialist also explains our team-based approach and our proven process to sellers, including our marketing strategies (more on this later).

Most sellers will never meet our *operations manager*, but the listing specialist is in constant contact with this person, who runs day-to-day operations for the team. Any issue that arises within the team—challenges, complaints, contract questions—goes to the operations manager. This role removes numerous headaches, chores, and concerns from the plate of the listing specialist, leaving him or her to devote all his or her energy to the listing.

Once the listing specialist has met with sellers, established pricing, and explained the process, the operations manager coordinates with a *stager*, who will assess the property and consult with sellers about how it should be staged. "Staging," as anyone who has ever visited a model home at a new development knows, involves coordinating furniture, space, artwork, accessories, landscaping, and other elements to show the home in its absolute best light.

Staging feels different from other home improvements because it's overseen by a professional stager, but it is most definitely a home improvement. In fact, it's the home improvement that offers the greatest return, the one that most impacts getting the highest price and fastest sale for a home. We will devote most of chapter 5 to staging, so I won't go into great depth here, but our stager advises sellers on which items to remove in order to cut down clutter and show rooms in their best light. The stager might also bring in outside furniture and accessories, as well as artwork. He or she might advise various changes in colors, paint, or general aesthetics, which we'll detail in chapter 6.

The listing specialist will discuss home improvements and staging with sellers. This team member knows more about interior design than our traditional agents, John and Jane, partly because of the high volume of houses we sell. The listing specialist knows what's in and what's selling, but leaving nothing to chance, we enlist yet another specialist, the stager, to handle staging.

With specialization comes skill, efficiency, and a high level of service—which is why it's the backbone of the dynamic agent's team approach. As a seller, the difference between having someone like John Smith tell you to "tidy up" or "brighten" the living room and having a professional trained in interior design expertly stage your house is the difference between getting hair advice from a gardener and getting it styled by Horst Rechelbacher, founder of Aveda. Buyers' standards for both photos and actual interiors have risen for reasons we'll discuss in chapter 5, but suffice it to say that the services of this expert have never been more necessary. Ultimately, they pay for themselves with higher sale prices and shorter market times.

When the staging work is done, the operations manager will schedule a time for the *photographer* to visit the house. Again, the difference between our approach to photos and that of Jane Smith can't be emphasized enough. Traditional agents often take photos themselves these days or have an assistant do it. If they say they're using a "professional photographer," they probably mean someone who also shoots weddings, portraits, parties, and whatever else he or she can line up.

We'll explore architectural photography in more depth in chapter 5, but it is a highly specialized discipline. The best fashion photographers and portraitists in the world are the first to admit they wouldn't know where to begin when it comes to photographing homes. Our photographers are meticulous about finding the optimal lighting, tone, color, and angles for each property. Setting up such shots is complex, and using a general photographer who doesn't specialize in this area isn't much different from having the agent snap pics on his phone.

As I mentioned before (and will mention again because it's so important to the sales effort), home buyers these days spend only a few seconds looking at a pic of each listing online before clicking the next one. Our goal as a team is to interrupt that pattern and have buyers stop at your home's photo. Our goal is always to win with presentation because these days, the first showing really occurs online, and buyers' first visit to the house is essentially the second showing. We have a professional stager and a top-notch photographer on the team because we know that they'll allow us to stop buyers in their tracks and win with presentation at that first online showing every time.

Once the photos are ready, our *marketing coordinator*—yet another specialist—prepares them for our multipronged marketing effort. In coordination with the listing specialist, this expert will select and prep photos for our launch event, the MLS, various websites, social media, direct mail, and other forms of marketing. Like other members of my team, the marketing coordinator is hard at work on a seller's listing behind the scenes. The seller's main point of contact is the listing specialist, and there's no need for him or her to talk to other team members who are working on this coordinated marketing effort.

As we'll discuss later, our marketing campaign will be tailored to the property, taking into account things like price point, location, and special features, but—and this is key—the presentation is always the same all-out effort by a dynamic agent. This is not the approach of the traditional Realtor®, who typically spends more time, effort, and money on presentation for higher-end properties.

We approach staging, photography, and presentation for a $200,000 home exactly as we do for a $3 million home. I'm offended by agents who worry less about presentation when the home is worth less—and sellers should be too. Is that family selling a $200,000 home worth less? Are their lives worth less? Is the trust they've put in an agent to sell their home worth less? I don't think so. In fact, lower-priced homes actually compete with a much larger pool of similar homes on the market, so great presentation is key. For every property, we leverage local agents whom we know are in touch with buyers interested in particular price points, locations, house styles, etc. For every property, we contact buyers on the proprietary lists that we generate from our website and use a sophisticated process to target buyers with messaging online and elsewhere.

We'll discuss this process more in chapter 7, but I want to point out here that using our own *web developer*—someone who helps us build and run a unique, dynamic website—is a critical difference from the traditional agent, who relies on a company website that he or she can't control. When John Smith pops a second-rate photo of your home on a giant corporate website, he might as well be taping a flyer to a light pole.

Our website is professional and easy to use, and all of our listings look stunning on it because we *always* win with presentation. This draws buyers to the site and builds traffic, so a home receives maximum exposure. Using our custom website, social media, Zillow, and other platforms, we can premarket homes while their owners are still getting them ready. Exposing a home to potential buyers even before it's officially listed is a great way to build momentum and postpones accumulating "days on market." We always want to minimize market time because each day on market erodes your power as a seller, and by embracing this "coming soon" phase and creating a pent-up demand and buzz for the property before it even goes live in the MLS, the sellers are essentially getting free advertising.

Because we control our website, we also can record key info from the buyers perusing it to create targeted lists. We track hundreds of buyers showing interest in your area. Our *administrative assistant* uses this info to generate custom lists of people who are either likely buyers themselves or know others who are, since most of us associate with people who have similar interests. The traditional agent does not have access to this sort of info nor the ability to generate a targeted list from the website they were given, which he or she has no control over.

As marketing gets underway, the listing specialist and marketing coordinator together contact our targeted list of buyers and the agents who work with them. Sellers tend to be most interested in reaching buyers, which is fine. They don't need to know about all the team members and various moving parts that go into reaching the entire market. The important thing is that by the time we launch, we have fully leveraged the agent community and all potential buyers in order to get a full-market response and create an environment that puts buyers in competition with each other, not with the seller. We'll explore the competitive sales environment in-depth in chapter 3.

The listing specialist presides over the launch, with assistance from a *runner, marketing coordinator,* and other team members. He or she monitors feedback, handles negotiations and offers, and is essentially the single point of contact for home sellers right up to the acceptance of an offer. The work of other team members happens behind the scenes. Lots of specialists are working on achieving a full-market response so that the sellers don't have to.

Whatever industry you may work in, you'll probably appreciate the principles behind the team approach I've presented here. No one would have wanted an iPhone actually assembled by Steve Jobs, though they were happy to have his vision behind the product. Would you buy a car completely assembled by one worker, who's perhaps great with engines but not brakes, or do you want one assembled by many workers, each an expert on his piece of the puzzle? Your doctor's office probably has a receptionist at the front desk, a nurse, and a facilities manager. We all want the doctor to stick to the part of the process where he or she can add the most value. You don't want the professional filling out forms at the front desk, drawing blood, and sweeping floors.

Traditional real estate is one of the few businesses where a single "professional" attempts to accomplish a wide range of tasks that he or she lacks the expertise to do well. Teams that sell dozens or hundreds of houses a year, however, understand that for the best-possible results, sellers need a professional stager to prepare their home, a real architectural photographer to photograph it, and a marketing coordinator to market it.

Real estate commissions often run tens of thousands of dollars, and sellers have every right to ask what that money is buying. Is the price tag attached to a dynamic agent leading a team of experts with hundreds of sales under his or her belt and coordinating a sophisticated sales effort to generate a full-market response . . . or to a solo agent who will list your home and pray it's one of the three or four he or she will sell (if it's a good year)?

CHAPTER 3

A COMPETITIVE SALES ENVIRONMENT

Recently, a couple called my team about a home they'd been trying to sell for three years. They'd listed the property, a high-end house in a desirable community, with another agent. That person did everything that the traditional agent, using the old "list-and-pray" approach, typically does. He put the listing in the MLS, stuck a sign in the yard, and had photographs taken. He dropped those pics onto the corporate website and ran ads. He took calls and made individual appointments, though for some reason, he didn't get many, and almost none toward the end.

Meanwhile, the property, a grand house worth significantly more than the average home even in this attractive neighborhood, languished on the market month after month, and then, literally, year after year. The owners, of course, never guessed that it would take so long to sell their house. The protracted effort disrupted their lives. It derailed their plans and became a financial drag. Instead of enjoying a quick sale that brought in cash, they suffered through an agonizingly slow one that cost several years' worth of property taxes, insurance, maintenance, and other unanticipated expenses.

When the listing expired with the previous agent, I took it on and sold the home in a little over two weeks. What does a dynamic agent do differently to turn a situation like this around? Well, many things—but if I had to put them under one umbrella, it would be this: I created a competitive sales environment. The other agent did not manage to do that. In fact, he did just the opposite.

One of several major reasons that the home saw few appointments and no offers in three years on market was that the agent priced it where nobody in that neighborhood was looking, too far past the point where homes in that area sell. He did this for "negotiating room," then prayed that a buyer would show up, essentially hoping that some other agent would sell the house for him. This was the strategy that he pursued for three years, while the home sat vacant and its owners lost a considerable sum.

When my team took over, we asked the sellers straight out, "What are you trying to achieve financially?" Their answer was about 12 percent below the price the previous agent had listed the house at. Their traditional agent's approach to "negotiating room" had done nothing but disinvite the market, guaranteeing that people wouldn't show up. Not only are savvy buyers put off by a property that's priced too high, but many buyers shopping for homes in the sellers' acceptable range never even saw the house. Online, where most buyers now begin browsing for homes, searches occur in brackets of $25,000, $50,000, and $100,000. Placing a home outside the appropriate bracket removes it from the search results that many target buyers will see. As we'll discuss in greater detail in chapter 8, with pricing, a misstep of even $1,000 can doom a property's online presence, a common outcome for agents guided more by misconceptions about "negotiating room" than an understanding of online real estate searches.

My team worked with the sellers and had them reprice the property so that it would be captured in home searches and occupy the appropriate "virtual shelf space." We'll explore this concept further in chapter 8, but imagine a store where a certain product is stacked on shelves by price, the least expensive versions on the bottom and the priciest on top. Shoppers' eyes immediately go to the shelf in their range. Excess "negotiating room" can shift the product—in this case, a home—to another shelf, where buyers in the appropriate bracket never see it.

The conversation with the sellers about a price adjustment wasn't easy—it never is. We first had to find out what the sellers really wanted for the property and then had to explain how search results work and why they were getting so few. Once the sellers understood our strategy, we were able to drop the price to 6 percent over what they wanted—not a major decrease but significant enough to get us into the right bracket.

Another difficult conversation followed the one about pricing, when we proposed that they stage the house. After three years of no movement, the wife in this couple was jaded by the whole sales process. She didn't see what difference staging would make and adamantly opposed it. Most agents would have backed off at that point, afraid to push the sellers. But confident in our dynamic-agent expertise, we nudged them. The house was empty and not showing well. We knew from our years of experience and thousands of sales that staging would make an immense difference.

Eventually, we got Mrs. Seller to agree and had a professional stager come out for a consultation. She temporarily brought in furniture that looked beautiful and matched the home's modern aesthetic. She also added artwork, carpets, lighting elements, and various accessories. The rooms immediately looked warmer and more inviting and, some readers will be surprised to hear, larger. As we'll discuss in chapter 5, buyers have trouble envisioning their furniture in empty rooms and gauging what will fit where. Staging takes the guesswork out of the process and presents buyers with a beautiful range of possibilities.

Our stager also optimized traffic flow, which is key to a successful launch, since our goal is to bring the entire market to the property at once. The stager considered what elements she wanted buyers to focus on and in what order and how she wanted them to move through the house.

Once the staging was complete, we brought in our photographer. The old photos, used in previous ads and online listings, were woefully inadequate. Our architectural photographer—a pro who has been photographing homes for decades—spent hours setting up shots, lighting rooms, and establishing the right conditions before even taking the first test shots. The results were truly stunning. Our goal is always to stop buyers mindlessly clicking through photos when they get to ours—to interrupt their pattern and to win with presentation every time.

Like expert staging and careful pricing, first-class photography is a key part of the dynamic agent's strategy for creating a competitive sales environment. Every element of our proven process is calculated to capture the attention of the entire market for a property, *all* buyers who want a home like this one. A lack of attention or expertise anywhere along the way can jeopardize the entire effort. This is why we take no chances when it comes to leveraging local agents to sell a home.

For the property in question, we did a careful analysis of market data to identify all local agents who seemed to be in touch with buyers looking for houses at this price point near this location. We then contacted each of those agents (no mere e-mail blast for something this important!) to invite them to our advance launch event. The launch was presented as an opportunity for agents to bring clients to a viewing of this unique property before a full-blown marketing effort got underway. From the first point of contact with agents, we stoke a spirit of competition regarding the property.

We also target buyers directly through our website. Dynamic agents *always* control their own websites. This allows us to collect data on prospective buyers browsing it for homes. For this property, we assembled a list of buyers who searched for this type of house, in this area, and at roughly our price point. As with the agents, each of these buyers received a personal call and an invitation to the advance launch—again presented as an insider opportunity to view the property before the full marketing effort got underway.

Online, we marketed the property strategically, targeting buyers with the demographic attributes that made them most likely to purchase. For instance, the fact that the house had several bedrooms on the same level made it especially well-suited to families with young children. We know from experience that this is a feature such families like, and we know how to use Google AdSense, Yahoo, Bing, etc. to target them. This type of advertising can get pricey, but it offers much more value per lead than blanket efforts, such as print ads in newspapers and magazines.

By the time of the launch event, we had created an intensely competitive selling environment. The home that had languished on the market for three years suddenly had many buyers perusing it—and each other. Our strategy of bringing the entire market to a staged home at one time is not only a model of efficiency and convenience, but it also spurs a sense of competition among potential buyers.

Remember our example of Apple from chapter 1? This sort of carefully crafted home launch is akin to Apple's release of the latest iPhone, when a blocks-long line outside the store creates a burning sense of urgency in consumers. A parallel example of this sort of competitive environment from the world of real estate is the grand opening of a developer's model. If you've ever attended such a grand opening, you probably noticed the way home buyers bustle about the meticulously staged model home, concerned that a certain floor plan might sell out or that another buyer will get the home they want.

The same palpable sense of urgency and excitement filled the air at our launch. Yes, buyers and agents munched hors d'oeuvres and sipped drinks, but they took the property—and all those other buyers—seriously. The same basic psychology and motivation at work on athletic fields and stock exchange trading floors comes into play. It's all right-brain, all very visceral. The emotions are flowing. The staging looks spectacular. Everything feels good. We all want to win, and we all have a fear of loss. In this atmosphere, a person begins to think, *I want this house. I could be happy here, and if I don't get it, I'm going to be unhappy. I don't want that couple to beat my family out. Or that one. Or her. Or . . .*"

Next thing you know, someone is purchasing a house he wasn't even ready to buy, but he went there because it felt good. The stunning photos worked on him. The staging wowed him. The home started to look like a trophy, and as more and more competing buyers showed up at our full-market launch, something primal kicked in.

The launch was a busy event for our team of specialists, who oversaw everything while gathering feedback from buyers. Their reaction to the beautiful staging and to the price was positive overall.

Someone will always grumble about the price point or the color in the living room, but this is the advantage of bringing the entire market to the house. Our listing specialist could gauge the full-market response and recommend adjustments, if any were needed, based on this valuable feedback rather than basing it on random opinions from individual appointments, as usually happens.

Our team tried to get every visitor registered at the launch, collecting his or her contact info, and our listing specialist called each person the next day to follow up. He asked all those who attended if they would be making an offer. He asked if they were interested in the home and why or why not. He solicited feedback on what they liked or didn't like about the property. This is invaluable information and a way to leverage the activity of a successful event.

We did not sell the house right at this launch event, though that frequently happens. Technically, we sold the house about two weeks later. The buyers, however, *did* come from the launch. They made an appointment for a second viewing when we followed up with them. We had quite a few individual showings in the two weeks between the launch and sale—probably more than the previous agent had scheduled in the previous three years—but the event essentially sold the property. With a properly structured launch like the one I just described, the dynamic agent will emerge either with the house sold or with a full-market response that tells us exactly what adjustments to make.

If we don't get an offer at the launch, we leverage the activity it generated. Yes, we scheduled individual showings the next week, but at each, we could say, "Hey, we don't have an offer yet, but we have had great interest in the house. The activity is hot on this one, so I suggest you write your offer as strongly as you can."

In this case, the home sold for its full list price in just over two weeks. That was 6 percent more than the sellers' acceptable price and significantly higher than the average home price in the neighborhood. This was not a "buyer's sale" by any means, despite the home's three-year sit on the market with the previous agent. It was a world-class marketing event that led to a successful sale, the type that has agents holding their heads high.

The sellers were holding *their* heads high, too. They were ecstatic. We'd had some touchy conversations about pricing, staging, and other items, but in the end, they trusted our expertise and got a phenomenal result when they'd all but given up hope. Most traditional agents would not have pushed back as we did in order to do what was best for the sale. The average agent would say, "You don't want to stage? You want to leave the price where it is? Okay, fine. Let me take the listing and stick my sign outside." We actually jeopardized our getting the listing by insisting on ideas that the seller was not immediately receptive to but that we knew were the best way to serve them. We articulated our strategy and thankfully, they listened, allowing us to make them a whole lot of money that they wouldn't otherwise have seen.

The sellers of this home hadn't sold a house in many years, so they were used to the traditional "list-and-pray" approach and a pricing scheme that included "negotiating room." The fact is that buyers these days don't need negotiating room. We'll discuss this in more depth when we get to pricing, in chapter 8, but what today's buyers need is *value*. It's no coincidence that sellers who build negotiating room into their homes need to negotiate—it's a function of the pricing. But buyers will buy where there's value, and they will pay market price if, like the one we've been discussing, the home is priced correctly.

Sometimes, for any of a host of reasons, the list price is off, or despite the best efforts of a Realtor® or a stager, some element of a property must be improved or altered if it's going to fetch the desired price. In these instances, getting true feedback from the entire market—not simply the trickle-in responses the average agent relies on—is vital. In the next chapter, I'll discuss the difference and explain how a dynamic agent gets and uses true feedback.

CHAPTER 4

GET FEEDBACK, NOT NOISE

I f you have ever sold a house using a traditional agent, it's quite possible you received no feedback at all while your home was on the market. Once they've listed a home, many old-school agents don't see communicating with sellers as an important part of their job until an offer comes in. Your agent probably promised to get the highest price the market would bear for your home in the shortest possible time. But how can sellers hope for the best from the market if they have no idea what the market thinks of their pricing, staging, curb appeal, location, etc.?

Getting *no* feedback, believe it or not, is a common scenario with real estate agents. The other possibility is what I call "trickle-in feedback." Most brokers have an automated feedback form they e-mail to buyers' agents who have brought clients by to see a home. The automated form asks questions such as: "Was the home priced well?" and "Is your buyer considering an offer?" There's also a spot at the bottom of the form where agents can jot down additional feedback. These responses can be helpful, but if they're an agent's only source of intelligence on a home, they're bound to fall short. They "trickle in" after appointments and, because of this, don't provide a timely comprehensive picture.

In the first scenario, sellers have nothing to work with. Does the market think the house is priced exorbitantly, reasonably, cheaply? Do buyers like the overall look or the new landscaping out front? What do people think of the colors in the newly painted upstairs or of all that taxidermy, borrowed from Uncle Frank to spruce up the den? Who knows? Not the agent—and certainly not the sellers.

In the second scenario, "feedback" trickles in after random appointments, but it's only so much noise, garbled and not especially useful. Sure, the Wednesday afternoon three o'clock appointment thought the house was overpriced by $20,000, but the Friday noon thought the asking price fair. The Monday morning hated the entire color scheme but no one else said that during the last two weeks. Of course, the last two weeks were slow, so . . .

Even if the sellers could track this chaotic trickle of data, what are they supposed to do with it? Should they reprice the house because some guy who saw it on Wednesday at three said so? Maybe he's right. Or maybe he skipped lunch that day and was feeling ornery. Should the sellers pay attention to Monday Morning's comments about the kitchen or Thursday Afternoon's about lightening up the finished basement? Who knows. These sorts of random opinions reflect the market about as well as a Magic 8 Ball reflects the future.

The sellers in the first scenario live in the dark—not a pleasant place to be when the biggest investment of your life hangs in the balance, but in the second scenario, the sellers might rush to adjust pricing and make improvements willy-nilly, with no real basis for doing so. True, there's some communication in the second scenario (much of it faulty), but if Realtors® took a Hippocratic Oath like doctors do, the first scenario would be the one to "do no harm." It does no good either, but still . . .

The dynamic agent utilizes a third option to produce valuable feedback that actually reflects the market as a whole and can be used by sellers in a practical way. In the last chapter, we discussed creating a competitive sales environment and the steps we take to bring the entire market to the home. This is a much better strategy than scheduling individual appointments, for many reasons. It's less disruptive for sellers, it's efficient, it stokes competition—and it yields genuine feedback.

Unlike most Realtors®, dynamic agents (such as my team and I) don't rely primarily on automated feedback forms. Instead, my team gets real-time data at the home's launch, when, because of our careful engineering, the entire market is represented. At this event, we can hear buyers' reactions firsthand. We listen to what they're feeling, observe what they're touching, note their objections and praise.

At the home I described in chapter 3—the one that stagnated for three years with another agent before I sold it in two weeks—our listing specialist took notes on the reactions of dozens of buyers at the launch. This is vital intelligence for a successful sale. How does such feedback differ from the traditional agent's? For starters, we get most of our information right from the buyers, rather than having it translated through a buyer's agent. After a host of showings, traditional agents sometimes have trouble even remembering which house they're providing feedback for. At a launch engineered to deliver a full-market response, on the other hand, we're gathering intelligence not just from the horse's mouth but while the horse is still in the stable. If everyone *oohs* and *ahs* over the kitchen but grumbles over the cramped family room, we feel the full power of the response. We note how buyers react to the space in real time.

The other important difference from the usual appointment-based strategy is that we are gauging the responses of twenty-five, thirty, or sometimes more than a hundred potential buyers all at once, at the outset of the sales effort. We collect and analyze the many responses we receive and then report this feedback to the sellers. This allows a dynamic agent to differentiate between the random naysayer who hates everything, complaining about the master bathroom that everyone else loved, and the couple who thought, along with fifteen other buyers, that the asking price is 10 to 15 percent too high. We can separate the wheat from the chaff, the valuable full-market feedback from the comments of random outliers. We're talking to the whole market at a single event.

When you have true full-market feedback as a seller, you can use it to make necessary adjustments with confidence. This is the heart of how to sell a home: can you truly capture a full-market response? Ideally, the feedback comes in the form of offers. If it doesn't, then you can make informed changes, knowing—not hoping blindly—that they'll work. Thirty buyers thought the property's asking price sounded fair? Keep it right where it is. Fourteen people questioned that tree limb scraping the roof? Spend the money to have it cut and eliminate that impediment. One person out of forty complained about the layout? Ignore him.

With our strategy, the market tells you what to do to sell your home, and it tells you early in the process, when your position as a seller is strongest. Sellers who wait until they've been on market for months to make changes encounter problems. For starters, their power has diminished by then. Over time, you cede negotiating power as a seller because with every passing day, you prove to the market you were unsuccessful at selling the home. Making adjustments when the listing is old and stale is not nearly as effective as changing things up front, when it's fresh and you have power.

Another problem with making changes over a period of months based on trickle-in feedback is that you never have an accurate snapshot of how the market feels about your home. Instead, you piece bits of information together over time, and especially in a changing market, the dated responses trickling in over several months might not be relevant to what you need today by the time they're decoded.

A dynamic strategy, by contrast, gives you true feedback from the entire market right away. Listen and act on it, and you will get the best-possible response from the market. Ignore that sort of feedback and well, you're back to list and pray.

I don't mean to suggest that sellers can adjust everything, even with a full-market response. Some items you can change and some you can't, but all feedback has value when it comes from the entire market. If everyone was dismayed by the chipped window frames and dead tree out front, perhaps those items need attention—and perhaps we need to revisit the issue of proper staging. If buyers' main concerns revolve around the location, those are obviously harder to address. You can fix a house, but you can't fix a neighborhood. But maybe we should adjust the price to compensate for its setting.

As I've pointed out, the commissions paid to Realtors® can run into tens of thousands of dollars. For that price, you deserve timely, full-market feedback, and it is the dynamic agent's job not only to report what the market says but also to interpret it. A good agent must read between the lines. If a number of buyers make vague comments such as "something just doesn't feel right in the house," what's the source of that sentiment?

Maybe the driveway needs power washing and the hardware on the front door is worn out, and those subtle details are creating a poor first impression. Those problems are easily solved for a few hundred dollars at the local home-improvement store. Perhaps the home is showing dark. People don't like homes that show dark, and it's up to the agent to realize that this is the problem and address it with the sellers. You can paint a dark room for less than $2,000, and lightening up a place full of dark blues and browns can have a major impact on how buyers respond. A $2,000 price reduction, on the other hand, has no impact whatsoever.

A dynamic agent shapes his or her sales strategy around this sort of feedback. In the example, the sellers can change the feel of the house for $2,000 early in the sales effort, when it will have maximum effect. And because we've brought the entire market to the home, this change stems from a broad-based response and not some random comment made at one appointment. This kind of adjustment makes much more sense than later having to make a price change, which would need to be in the tens of thousands of dollars to have any real impact.

In addition to being an astute interpreter of what the market says, a dynamic agent also offers creative responses to feedback. At one property that we recently sold, my team kept hearing at the launch that the home should have an additional bedroom, given the price point. Changing the price to compensate would have cost tens of thousands of dollars. Instead, we advised the sellers to build in a loft, which essentially added an extra bedroom for much less than a price reduction would have cost. The adjustment worked, and the home sold. Often, we can find innovative ways to deal with things that seem unchangeable, which is always preferable to a price reduction.

Collecting true feedback is often just as difficult as addressing it creatively. You need an agent who's not afraid to push and get real, actionable intelligence, because people are generally polite. I can't count how many times I've shown a house and the buyers loved it—genuinely thought it was great—but at first decided not to make an offer. They didn't have a single negative thing to say—until nudged. Why aren't you making an offer, honestly? "Well, the homes here seem a little too close together . . . We wanted a slightly more open floor plan . . . The view isn't as good as we'd hoped it would be . . ." We obviously can't move the homes farther apart or improve the view. If after pushing, the agent gets this sort of feedback, he or she should realize that it relates back to price even though that's not the buyer's explicit objection.

Very few agents gather this sort of feedback or know how to use it creatively, as I'm describing, but if they do, the clients then have two options. They can adjust and sell or block their ears and convince themselves that everyone else is wrong and they're right. The most sophisticated, representative feedback is useless if we don't use it strategically.

Sellers are sometimes reluctant to react to feedback, though, because having sold homes under the list-and-pray regime, they understandably don't put much stock in it. They don't realize that the kind of feedback my team supplies means something completely different. They don't know that there's a feedback problem in residential real estate, because their agent uses the same trickle-in approach that Realtors® have always used. To be fair, agents are equally unaware that the inherited system they use is badly broken. Many probably sense that it yields poor results, but as disciples of the list-and-pray method, they don't know any other way of doing things. A new breed of dynamic agent does.

CHAPTER 5

STAGING FOR SUCCESS

H ow we live in a home and how we sell it are completely different things. Your place might be beautiful, even stunning, the kind everyone compliments when they visit, but that doesn't eliminate the need for staging when you put it on the market. Most of us decorate our homes for comfort, not flair. We want them functional and livable, but photos of a room that feels great for movie watching or the kids' playtime might rate somewhere between dull and invisible in the court of online opinion.

You shouldn't be offended by this, no matter how much you love your house. Even supermodels blend into the crowd when they pop out for coffee, sans shower, after a late night. They don't live their daily lives with makeup artists, perfect lighting, and $10,000 gowns. But the advertising industry understands on an acute level how to give them a *look* that will sell once they're on camera.

Think of your home the same way: as a potentially gorgeous model who has one look for daily living and another for marketing. Your house has to win a beauty pageant online, and that takes work. Perhaps your living room is decked out in the earth tones you love.

Everyone tells you it's comfortable and cozy. That's terrific, and I'm glad it has served you well, but it's my job to inform you that in a photo online, those elements will blend together. The living room that's so comfortable in real life will become a mere blur for buyers browsing a real estate website, and when you're on market, their reaction is all that matters.

Not so long ago, sellers only had to worry about how a house looked when buyers arrived for the first showing. Home shoppers perhaps saw a black-and-white newspaper ad before they paid a visit, but the ad contained only one or two pics of the house, and the print quality was so poor that it didn't much matter. Today, the first showing is online, where buyers can scan dozens of high-resolution photos. Our buyers can view homes remotely, with a full 3-D virtual-reality experience, an interface gaining in popularity as big tech companies like Google and Apple focus on it. You must win with presentation because buyers are viewing your home in a multitude of ways before they ever reach the front door.

THE IMPORTANCE OF PHOTOGRAPHY

The starting point for any discussion of staging then is photography. As I have pointed out, studies show that online real estate shoppers typically spend three to five seconds on each photo when browsing. Looking at dozens, possibly hundreds, of housing photos in one sitting turns even the most attentive home buyer into something of a zombie. You need to win buyers over instantly, within seconds, or—click—they're on to the next house.

My team puts an enormous amount of energy into photography because we understand how buyers behave. We use only the best architectural photographers. Yes, we could save a lot of money by hiring cheaper photographers or, as many agents do, snapping some pics ourselves, but high-quality photographs pay for themselves with faster sales and higher prices. Crisp, beautiful photography is vital to getting a full-market response. It's hard to have the entire market represented at a launch when half of it is clicking past second-rate photos.

Our photographers can spend hours setting up shots, manipulating interior lighting, figuring out the best times of day for shooting exteriors, taking hundreds of photos to produce that single perfect frame. They understand that if you have mere seconds on people's computer screens, that the photo better jump out and make buyers pause. Keep in mind that most buyers didn't start looking for a home yesterday. Many shopped for months before they got to your listing. They're flipping through home after home, photo after photo, and they're going fast. They've seen so many properties that they begin blending and blurring. Soon, they can't tell one from the next.

We win with presentation every time because we know how to interrupt this pattern. Consider my example of the earth-tone room. Though the room looks great when you're in it, there's nothing to grab you in a photo. We stage it with accessories, new artwork, pillows that accent the sofa, bright plates in a table setting for color—and that makes the room pop. Through staging and top-quality photography, we force buyers to linger over photos because ours look so much better than all the others.

I'm saying "we" here, but as I highlighted in chapter 2, when I sell a house, I turn this job over to a professional stager who is trained in interior design and does nothing else. Stagers study what's in vogue. They track trends and know what people want to see. They know exactly what elements will match the style of a particular home, and they're experts in buyers' psychology.

STAGE FOR YOUR MARKET

Stagers also consider who the most likely buyer of a property is and stage accordingly. If the target demographic is retirees in their sixties, the stager might recommend changing all the white walls and white woodwork because such buyers won't find this look appealing. If, on the other hand, the target audience is people in their midthirties, who are online pinning things to their Pinterest boards every day, they might love all that white.

What other types of changes do stagers make? Well, homeowners are often surprised to learn that much of the stager's work involves addition by subtraction. At the start of this chapter, I noted that the way that you live in a home isn't necessarily the way to sell it. Our lifestyles generally require more "stuff" than we want, present when it's time to show a home to buyers. Often, more than 50 percent of the furniture, accessories, knickknacks, etc. in a home must go, and the stager is an expert in making such cuts. As a rule, I advise home sellers who don't use the services of a stager to remove half the belongings from a house when selling. We want to draw buyers' eyes to the gleaming hardwood floors, light-filled windows, and other features of the home and not to the belongings in it. It's the home we're selling, so eliminating the things that distract from it is vital.

Much of the removal simply addresses clutter, but some items might also be taken out or changed because they are too limiting. A quirky piece of furniture that the owners love might not appeal to many buyers. Though the nautical theme in the den reflects years of careful collecting, it needs toning down for the landlubbers seeing the house. Stagers aim for wide appeal, so anything that unduly narrows the home's audience must go. An old school of thought included family photos in this category, but I think a few family pics here and there add warmth and are usually more help than hindrance. If there are so many family photos that it's hard for a buyer to imagine his own family in the space, then we do need to depersonalize it a bit.

The stager will also make additions. These might include furniture, especially if the home is vacant, but most staging involves smaller items, accessories, and impactful design changes most lay people wouldn't consider. No detail is neglected when stagers turn their expert eyes on a home. What sorts of towels will work best in the guest bathroom? What kinds of flowers will complement the colors in the family room? What style of vase should they be in? From baskets to soap dishes to full-blown works of art, the stager will bring in a myriad of items to transform a home and show it in the best-possible light in both pictures and live presentations.

Homeowners can spruce up homes themselves, of course, but not even those with good design sense have the impact of a professional stager. For instance, most sellers wouldn't give much, if any, thought to closets. There's no way to change their size, and they all contain clothes and shoes, so who cares how the closets look? Well, the stager does. The closets can't be empty—buyers must have a sense of what they can fit inside—but they can't be jammed full of stuff either. Otherwise, the buyer immediately says, "Gee, honey, there just doesn't seem to be enough room here." When you open a closet door, and everything is in orderly rows and fits comfortably, buyers think, *Hey, there's plenty of room in this house, plenty of storage.*

The same holds true for the kitchen pantry and cabinets. The exact same kitchen can appear spacious, with plenty of storage, or crammed, with not nearly enough room, depending on how well it is staged. Buyers are very visual, so it's all about making a good first impression.

A SCIENCE AND AN ART

The stager understands not just décor but also buyers and their thought processes in a way that homeowners don't. Staging is where psychology meets design—both as a science and an art. The stager controls where people's eyes land when they walk through a door and what lines their sight then follows. He or she controls how visitors flow through and react to the space, though buyers are generally unaware that they're being influenced in this way.

When my team plans a launch that might attract twenty-five, thirty, forty buyers, all competing with each other, the stager plans for that traffic, too. They rearrange furniture to optimize the flow of people. Potential logjams where buyers might get stuck are removed, and logical, comfortable routes are established.

Consider your local grocery store and how carefully it has been staged to sell. You enter on one side in a very controlled manner and are steered quite strategically through various stands and down an aisle. We've all had the experience of reaching an "endcap," those displays at the end of the row where things are staged to sell, and dropping something in the shopping cart because it caught our eye. Who hasn't succumbed to the impulse buy at checkout? Stagers apply the same sort of strategy to make your home as attractive and salable as possible.

Stagers are artists, but they also analyze your space with the cool, objective eye of an outsider. This is invaluable because sellers often have trouble suspending their emotional attachment to a home when preparing it for sale, and that can hurt the marketing effort. They often think, *This painting needs to be there because we love it,* or *I built this in the house, so it has to stay.* The stager can help the sellers take a step back and look at things more objectively. Getting an expert's take on what should stay, go, or get changed is vital.

Paradoxically, the stager's analytical, unemotional approach is all about producing an emotional response in home buyers. When they view your home, you want buyers to see it from a "right-brain," or emotional, perspective. You want buyers using the left side of their brain, which involves numbers and negotiation, as little as possible. The right side of the brain tells them that the home feels good, looks good, smells good. The place needs to be inviting in visceral ways because getting those positive emotions flowing leads to the best and highest response.

Many of the elements of staging that we've discussed help to create that emotional state in prospective buyers. We remove some limiting items because they get in the way of the emotional response. That giant nude self-portrait by the sellers' son, the amateur painter? The stager knows what she's doing when she gets rid of it, the same as when she accessorizes to stir feeling. The perfectly coordinated towels in the bathroom, the art deco sconces in the den, the ornate vase of midnight-blue irises on the mahogany coffee table: these are all calculated to produce particular emotional responses.

"Wow" is the frequent response of buyers viewing well-staged rooms. "This is *nice*. Awesome." The responses can be vague— sometimes no more than the beaming look a couple exchanges on entering a room—because buyers aren't exactly sure why the well-staged home feels so *right. I don't know,* they think later, *the others were nice, but that one just felt good.* It felt good, I can tell you from years of experience and thousands of sales, because a professional stager sweated every detail to produce an emotional response. That "wow" response can mean tens of thousands of additional dollars in buyers' offers.

Homes that aren't staged, or aren't staged well, produce very different comments. "Hey honey, what do you think? Would our sofa fit here? That one's an odd length, so I'm not sure about ours . . . Would we put it here or there?" If the home is vacant, buyers start debating where to place the bed and whether or not there's enough room for their chairs. "Is this living room smaller than ours, or does it just feel that way because they have more stuff?" "What would be a better color for this room?" You know you've lost the battle of the emotions when the tape measures come out and prospective buyers start jotting numbers. People pacing the room to measure off feet will never yield as much money at sale as the couple who would have walked into that same room if it were staged, smiled at each other, and simply said, "Wow." I can usually tell within minutes of buyers walking in the door if they'll make an offer.

Buyers need to feel good, and they need to justify their purchase, and staging helps them do that. They feel happy and comfortable in the space, and the wife says to the husband, or vice versa, "I could see us raising our family here. This feels like the right house." Buyers have a much harder time imagining themselves in the home that isn't staged. As a seller, you want to leave as little as possible to the buyer's imagination.

PEOPLE PACING THE ROOM TO MEASURE OFF FEET WILL NEVER YIELD AS MUCH MONEY AT SALE AS THE COUPLE WHO WOULD HAVE WALKED INTO THAT SAME ROOM IF IT WERE STAGED, SMILED AT EACH OTHER, AND SIMPLY SAID, "WOW." I CAN USUALLY TELL WITHIN MINUTES OF BUYERS WALKING IN THE DOOR IF THEY'LL MAKE AN OFFER.

Today's consumers expect to be catered to in this way. They are more demanding, more educated, and a little more high maintenance. They watch *Flip This House* on high-definition TV and the DIY Network. They track the latest home trends on Pinterest and browse hot designs on Houzz. They're fed, essentially, a fantasy world on TV and the Internet, and they judge every house by these standards. When homes don't live up to their ideal, the left side of the brain kicks in—the thinking side. They start calculating how much it would cost to make your house look like one of those HGTV homes, but that's not where you want their focus. When a home is staged, buyers typically feel that moving in wouldn't require much work, and as a seller, you want them to see the place as move-in ready or as close to that condition as possible.

Many consumers today also have been to new developments—perhaps you have, too—and all the big builders these days have staged model homes at their communities. Companies like Ryland, Pulte, Lennar, and Cal Atlantic, which spend a small fortune analyzing what buyers want, stage homes for all the reasons we've discussed. The model homes at their new communities are meticulously crafted, which is why consumers at new developments often want to purchase the models (they're said to be the best houses). If you're selling an existing home, this is your competition. Your home needs to look every bit as attractive as that builder's model, and this will only happen with the expertise of a professional stager—the same professional the builder used on his.

LEAVE IT TO THE PROFESSIONALS

We live in the golden age of DIY, and sellers sometimes attempt to stage their homes themselves. Trying this is better than doing nothing, but unless you're an interior designer or a professional stager, you won't get the same results. You trust your legal work to a qualified attorney. If you have bunions, you go to a podiatrist. And odds are, you don't fix your own car. I recommend the same strategy when it comes to staging. Using a firm that employs professionals results in faster sales and higher prices, so in a sense, the service pays for itself.

USING A FIRM THAT EMPLOYS PROFESSIONALS RESULTS IN FASTER SALES AND HIGHER PRICES, SO IN A SENSE, THE SERVICE PAYS FOR ITSELF.

Sellers can be reluctant about staging if they don't understand the process. As I have pointed out, much of the work—*most* of it, at many houses—simply involves removing items to declutter the home. Stagers typically work on this effort with sellers. The homeowners typically do this work (the stager can remove items, too, for a fee, if this is requested), and the stager then brings in any necessary accessories, and arranges the existing furniture.

The additions might include new furniture, especially if the home is empty, but oftentimes, smaller items suffice—soap dishes, towels, placemats, flowers, a vase. Homeowners who have moved out, leaving the vacated house clean and empty, sometimes think this is the ideal way to sell it. After all, the place surely looks bigger without a stick of furniture in it. Right? Wrong! I can tell you unequivocally that this is not true. Clutter makes rooms feel small, but homes actually look bigger when elegantly furnished. As I pointed out earlier, homeowners should leave as little as possible to the buyers' imaginations. An empty house makes them imagine everything, so the home most definitely needs the services of a good stager if it's going to sell for top dollar.

The sellers' portion of the staging work could take three days, or a little longer, depending on what needs to be removed, but with a professional stager's guidance, the work should be fast and painless. The stager's initial visit doesn't take long, and the actual staging of the property lasts anywhere from half a day to two days (possibly longer, if, for instance, the property is enormous or a hoarder house).

Stagers ideally do their portion of the work a week or so before we put the home on the market, but it's a good idea for homeowners to contact an agent as soon as they decide to sell, even if that's six months or more before they want to list the home. Removing items can be time consuming, so if I can set up a staging consultation early in the process, this often saves sellers stress, allowing them to work at an easier pace.

Whether you are selling next week or in two years, get a professional agent's opinion right away so that you don't replace the wrong things or spend money on areas that don't need it. Homeowners who decide to sell and don't contact an agent for many months also tend to decide on their own which items should stay or go. They begin painting and making repairs and various changes. Unfortunately, they do this without much knowledge of what buyers want, what's "in" at the moment, or how things will pop visually in online photos. Getting the input of a dynamic agent and his or her expert stager can save sellers from making bad choices and creating work for themselves later. I've had countless conversations in which I have had to gently point out to sellers that some design change they thought of as an improvement is doing more harm than good.

Sellers don't have to stage, of course—but they should if they want the most possible money for their home. Nothing you can do to your property will have a greater impact. Unlike repairs and improvements, which upgrade one small area, staging elevates the entire property. It results in better photos, brings more people to your home, and enhances their experience once they get there. Staging is the biggest win you can have, and it's proven by our hundreds of home sales as well as by every national homebuilder—companies that know how to get the most for a property. Leveraged by a dynamic agent who understands marketing and how to get your home noticed online, staging becomes an invaluable part of the process building to a full-market response.

CHAPTER 6

EASY WINS: SIMPLE IMPROVEMENTS WITH BIG PAYOFFS

My purpose in this book is not to show you how to flip your house. I'm not going to explain how to tear your kitchen apart and build a new one or how to install new plumbing. When it comes to selling your home, it's best to think of improvements as part of the *presentation* process and prioritize them accordingly. The question is: Where can you find the easy wins that yield big results?

The first answer is always *deferred maintenance*.

Why? I prioritize deferred maintenance not because it will get you more than the market average for your home but because it will prevent you from getting penalized on price. If the problems you've put off for years are not taken care of, you will sell your home for less than it's really worth.

What is "deferred maintenance?" It includes everything from that old corroded doorknob to the leaky roof to the cracked window.

It's the stuff buyers expect to have in good working order, and if it isn't, they understandably expect a lower price.

It's important for sellers to realize that addressing deferred maintenance simply brings the property back to an acceptable level. They don't always know this. Not long ago, I worked with homeowners who had put a new roof on their house a couple of years earlier. They thought this would boost its value compared to similar houses nearby. I had to explain that their buyers would expect a roof that wasn't leaking and half rotted. The fact that the sellers had replaced a leaky roof with one in good working order was not going to prompt a higher price; it would simply avoid a lower one. The uniform appraisal report used in real estate does not contain line items for roofs, counters, or flooring. This is because no one gives credit for such items—though they will take credit away if such items aren't in good condition, noting any problems in the "miscellaneous" section of the form.

In addition to deferred maintenance, sellers should consider the improvements that will have the biggest impact on potential buyers. These don't have to be large or expensive elements. Take something simple, like the knob on your front door. It works well enough that you haven't thought of it as deferred maintenance, but perhaps it's old and beat up, a little loose and corroded. But so what? It's just a doorknob. Who cares?

You should.

Buyers might not remember the doorknob or think that they care about it either, but it has an effect just the same. The doorknob is literally the first thing that a buyer makes physical contact with at a home. When you have an old, corroded doorknob versus a new, shiny one, it creates a very different experience for the buyer. Whether they know it or not, buyers grabbing that chipped, rattling doorknob are already forming a judgment. Subconsciously, they have categorized the house as somehow shabby or subpar before they even set foot inside. You're allowing a buyer to experience your home through a less-than-ideal lens, when making the door look *right* would only have cost $100 or $150. That sort of small investment—what I sometimes call "Band-Aid fixes" because they're affordable but have high impact—gets you a buyer walking in, not with judgment, but with an open mind and ready to experience all that the home has to offer. These Band-Aid fixes tend to usually be paint, flooring, and fixtures.

I'm not sure who first said "the devil is in the details," but he or she might have been a real estate agent. Details like that doorknob matter immensely to your bottom line. When you're negotiating an asset worth hundreds of thousands, if not millions of dollars, the value is fluid and not predetermined to the penny. The price falls within a probable range and can move thousands of dollars, or even tens of thousands, in either direction. Having a buyer walk into a home with a mind-set that tilts more toward the positive or negative because of details like that doorknob can make a difference of many thousands of dollars when the offer comes in.

This is why first impressions are so important. To make the point, I often tell the story of a home I was selling some years ago. All of the feedback we got after the grand opening included positive comments about the high ceilings in this house. "We love the high ceilings—such a feeling of space," people kept remarking. I wondered what they were talking about. The ceilings weren't high at all—under nine feet in every room. When I returned to the house, though, I realized that the entryway *did* have high ceilings, of fifteen to eighteen feet. The buyers had judged the home as they entered it, and that initial experience remained with them as they viewed the rest of the property.

This sort of positive initial judgment is what you want, not the negative perception of the buyer who feels slightly dirty just touching an old crummy doorknob. That tainted outlook can carry through a viewing just as powerfully as the perception of high ceilings did in my example. Think of other elements of the property that might have similar negative effects. Perhaps the driveway is grimy and discolored, some pieces of siding are rotting, or the grout around the foyer tile is discolored. Power washing a driveway or regrouting is simple and cheap, but these sorts of improvements can have an outsized impression on buyers. Their whole experience of the property changes with such details. This is what I mean by "easy wins"—the home improvements that allow small investments to yield big results.

Deciding what to improve is important, but it's equally important to spend the money on improvements up front, when you'll get marketing value for those dollars. The worst mistake sellers can make is to acknowledge that, yes, their carpet is totally shot. Yes, it's twenty years old, and they raised three children on it. They know this, and so they decide to credit buyers $2,000 to allow them to replace the carpeting after closing. Problem solved, right?

Wrong!

This is one of the worst mistakes sellers can make. In offering a credit, they are spending all of the money for an improvement and getting none of the benefit. Sure, buyers will take the credit, but they're still experiencing the home by walking across icky carpeting. The logical parts of their brains might note the credit and discount the ratty carpeting, but they can't *actually* discount it. Subconsciously or consciously, they will be affected by that shabby surface under their feet. Judgment is setting in.

Credits are usually a terrible idea, no matter what they're for. Your home truly needs a paint job? Instead of crediting $3,000 for paint, have it painted. You're spending the money with the credit, just as if you hired a contractor, but potential buyers still experience the dingy walls, which will affect the final price, perhaps by many thousands of dollars. This is the worst of all worlds—all of the expense with none of the payoff.

It's no secret among Realtors® that buyers have a hard time imagining the future. This is why we devoted chapter 5 to staging. Don't leave that new carpeting or fresh paint to the buyers' imagination. Because they can't imagine it! Give them the vision, and present it as beautifully as you can. Also, remember that the first showing today occurs online, so many buyers will never click through for more info and find out about credits for carpeting or paint. Others who do find out won't want the hassle of making such improvements later. Taking care of these cosmetic items is the way to get the highest price the market will bear for your home and to sell it in the shortest possible time.

Sellers avoiding improvements often cling to the notion that they can't predict what flooring or paint colors the buyers will want. What if they pick the wrong material or colors? Are they supposed to just rely on their gut?

RELYING ON "GUT" INSTINCTS MEANS YOU'VE GIVEN UP THINKING, AND SELLERS SHOULD NEVER DO THAT.

Absolutely not. Relying on "gut" instincts means you've given up thinking, and sellers should never do that. Instead, get a professional dynamic agent to the house, one with a proven track record and dozens if not hundreds of annual sales under his or her belt. An agent doing that sort of volume is completely in tune with what the market wants. In coordination with a professional stager, the agent will help you spend home-improvement dollars on what the majority of the market wants. This might not be what the sellers want, but—and this is important—the sellers' personal predilections are irrelevant now. They're not improving a home to live in, they're assembling a showroom, just as the national homebuilders do with their staged models.

Sellers are right to question their own choices of colors, carpet, and other improvements. The answer, however, is not to give credits for improvements but to have a professional agent out for a consultation as soon as possible. Whether the home is going on the market in six months, a year, or eighteen months from now, consulting with a good agent right away can make clear just what buyers want in that sort of home in that particular market. This will help shorten market time, maximize price, and avoid mistakes.

I can't tell you how many times I walk into homes and the sellers show off how they freshly painted, and I have to smile and gently inform them that those colors are perfect—for 2003. As I wrote in the last chapter, a seller in this situation could save considerable money and hassle by contacting me sooner to understand what colors are in or will appeal to particular buyers. I can assess such improvements with confidence because I sell enough homes to know. Agents who aren't selling *at least* one home a week might be as out of touch with what the market wants as the homeowners are, in which case the sellers are spending a lot of money in commissions for very little in return.

Experienced agents can save sellers money and hassle in other ways, too. Let's say the oven isn't working correctly, or the ice maker is broken. For items like these, I tell sellers that a credit is fine. I know, I just said credits were a bad idea, but here, we aren't violating my rule: *if you're spending the money anyway, always get marketing value.* The reality is that when all those buyers walk through the property at your grand opening, they aren't going to bake cookies, so the broken oven won't affect the experience. Disclose the problem, absolutely, but you don't need to spend on it up front. It's important to know this because you have limited dollars to bring a property to market, so you must prioritize. Things that won't affect the viewing experience for buyers can wait.

Some improvements might enhance the viewing experience but are still a bad idea because they won't give enough bang for the buck. Consulted early, I often save homeowners significant sums they planned to spend on major home improvements. Frequently, I see homeowners deciding to sell and thinking, *Well, maybe we'll remodel the bathroom or part of the kitchen.*

They think this will get them full, turn-key value for the house, but this sort of improvement is tricky. If the sellers haven't touched the home in thirty years and suddenly want to put a little money into the kitchen or bath, for example, I advise that they either become true home-flippers and rehab the place thoroughly, or simply clean it, address deferred maintenance, stage it—and put the rest of that money back in their pockets. Short of renovating the entire property, they won't be able to sell it for turn-key value. Spending thousands on a bathroom or kitchen won't increase the price enough to make it worth the expense and hassle.

Often, when such sellers fix the master bathroom, they aren't changing the value, as they think; they're just confusing the market. Part of the house is upgraded and part isn't, and buyers aren't sure what to make of that. Again, it's important to consult a qualified agent early on. I work in some neighborhoods where the housing is newer, and even the lowest-priced properties have granite counters and high-end finishes. In such niches, if you have the only house with 1980s tile, some buyers will lower their estimate of the value because of that. Other buyers won't even consider the house because they don't want to take on such improvements themselves. In this situation, you might as well upgrade.

At other homes, the owners might already have upgraded most of the property except for a dated bathroom. In that case, I also would advise renovating the bathroom because it needs to join the rest of the home. Every case is different, however, and an experienced agent doing enough volume to truly understand the market can help you make those tough calls.

I'll finish this chapter with some of my favorite "easy wins," the affordable home improvements that offer big bang for the buck. These are things that don't take much time, money, or work but bring returns on your initial investments in multiples of four, five, even ten at closing time. They also cut down on market time and help foster the competitive environment that's at the heart of my selling strategy.

THE MAGNIFICENT 7: THE EASIEST WINS WITH THE BIGGEST RETURNS

FRONT DOOR. In terms of rate of return on investment (RRI), I would argue that it's tough to beat improving that crappy front door. What does it take to make the front door and its attendant hardware truly beautiful and inviting? Usually $150 is more than enough, but because of its prominence, this improvement could boost the home's value by $1,500 or more. The return will likely be ten times the investment, while sinking $15,000 into a kitchen might bring back less than $20,000 at closing time.

LANDSCAPING. This is more involved than the front door but also ranks high in terms of first impressions. Homeowners often want to cut down on water use either because of expense or environmental concerns. That's understandable, though I can tell you as an agent selling hundreds of homes, people love grass. It photographs better, sells the home faster, and for those worried about cost or upkeep, it quickly becomes the buyer's responsibility. Sellers opposed to grass can use mulch, gravel, rocks, and other landscape elements, but they must look intentional. You don't have to hire an expensive landscape architect, but you do have to plan the yard. Weeds won't sell.

WINDOWS. No, don't install new windows, unless that's absolutely necessary. Instead, remove the screens and thoroughly clean all glass. This costs nothing and has a huge effect. Your rooms suddenly will be flooded with natural light. They'll instantly look bigger and feel better. (Make sure to keep the screens in a safe out-of-the-way place—your buyer will want them later.) If you have wood windows that are starting to look like they may be weathered from years of condensation, then you could have a professional sand and stain them, which will freshen up the look of the windows.

BASEBOARDS. You have probably ignored them for twenty years. It's time to pay attention. Make sure that they're clean and freshly painted, with chips and nicks filled in or touched-up. They need to look sharp. Savvy buyers use baseboards as an indicator of how well a property has been maintained, but even those who don't subconsciously register dingy, banged-up baseboards, which can detract from an otherwise beautiful room.

FLOORING. This is a big one. Nearly every house I see needs at least some flooring replaced because, well, people live in their homes.

Flooring takes a beating. Just as the doorknob is the thing *first* touched, flooring is the thing *most* touched. The buyer is in contact with it the entire time he's viewing the property, so it has to look and feel right. Again, consult your Realtor® before replacing it. I've encountered buyers, for example, who proudly show me all the new carpeting they installed to prepare their homes for sale, when the market would have preferred hard surfaces. If you have a dog, you may need to look at getting the floor refinished rather than replaced to fix the scratches your dog has left on the flooring.

PAINTING. Around 80 percent of a house is basically flooring and paint, if you think about it. This is how we encounter the space—as floors and walls. Painting is not expensive and offers a terrific return. Take a drab house that's showing terribly—and with $2,000 worth of paint later, it not only feels much better, its value typically has increased by well over $2,000.

STAGING. We saved for last the number-one home improvement that any homeowner can possibly do. Staging upgrades *the entire property,* with minimal cost and huge return. The typical return on staging is somewhere in the neighborhood of four to six times the investment, which means it's not only free, but at the end of the day, it actually makes you money. A perfectly clean house, where deferred maintenance has been addressed, where everything looks alive and intentional, and a professional stager has worked his or her magic has an astonishing effect on buyers. Replacing simple items such as light fixtures, interior door knobs, and cabinet hardware can completely alter the ambience in a house. Even old elements somehow look newer. Everything feels *right,* and the same home unstaged invariably would sell for a lower price, with a longer market time.

CHAPTER 7

MARKETING THAT STAYS ON TARGET

J ohn and Jane Smith, the traditional agents I've been referencing throughout this book, think of the financial side of selling in terms of their commissions. Their strategy, as I've pointed out, involves little more than putting a listing in the MLS and sticking a sign in a yard. They focus on the commission because it represents a substantial financial reward for a comparatively small amount of work, which the average agent needs to survive when they are only selling around four homes per year.

My focus as a dynamic agent is on marketing dollars because, first of all, by contracting to pay me a fee if I sell your home, you basically are entrusting me with a substantial marketing budget. Second, marketing a home in an effective, targeted way these days— using social media, online ads, big data, proprietary lists, direct mail, and other methods—is complex and quite expensive.

Sellers often think that the Internet has made selling homes less pricey, and the traditional agent, who doesn't know any better, might agree. In fact, marketing housing well has grown more expensive.

Data has become much more defined; an agent who knows how to use it to target buyers can do so much more efficiently, but that reach has a price tag.

What sort of "data" am I talking about? The best way to think of it might be in terms of our online footprints. Google, Yahoo, Facebook, Snapchat, and various other online entities collect data on their users. If you've looked up information about shoes online, for instance, you'll notice that ads from shoe companies start popping up wherever you turn. Suddenly your Facebook feed is rife with sponsored posts about the latest pumps or loafers.

That's just the tip of the data iceberg, as you probably know from Internet strategies in your own industries or simply from shopping online. As you're shopping, browsing, and posting, you're creating an online digital footprint that tells marketers where you shop and hang out, whether you're single or married, how much you make, and how many kids you have. They know your credit score, where you travel, and if you're thinking of moving. They probably even have a pretty good estimate of the kind of mortgage you can get preapproved for.

Companies like Google and Facebook use this data to target consumers in unprecedented ways. They don't actually sell consumers' personal information to marketers, but they allow marketers like me to create ads within their platforms that will, for example, target people of a certain age, people who are thinking of moving, and people who earn over a certain income.

If I determine that one likely buyer profile for a property is married men over sixty who golf and earn at least $250,000 a year, I can now target those consumers, creating ads that will show up in their newsfeeds or browsers. If I list a house that has three or four bedrooms on a single level, I know from the many homes I've sold in the last year that this type of property will appeal to families with younger children. I can pay online to target those potential buyers. This isn't cheap, but at least I know I'm spending our marketing dollars wisely. Ads in newspapers and magazines aren't cheap either—and they offer no real targeting for sellers.

The ability to tap into all of this relevant data and only show your home to people who are most-likely buyers, as opposed to people just casting a wide net is a very defined approach to marketing that gives sellers an incredible advantage—provided their agent understands it. Beware of the agent who touts the benefits of his or her corporate brokerage website. Your presence on such a site will be essentially free—and you'll certainly get what you pay for. The giant corporate real estate website is a blunt instrument. It doesn't target buyers, and because your agent doesn't control the site, he or she can't harvest helpful data about who sees your listing there, assuming he or she even understands the importance of such efforts.

The same is true for the MLS. Of course, your listing should be in the MLS, but that's little more than a starting point, and agents who rely on this sort of "marketing" to sell your home are living in another decade. They will tell you that in addition to putting your home in the MLS, they will list it on "hundreds of websites." Again, don't be impressed by this. Such syndication of listings is automatic online. It requires no work on the agent's part and simply means that a robot will indiscriminately feed your property listing to various sites, with no strategy whatsoever. My targeted approach is as different from this one as a scalpel from a chainsaw.

In the hands of the traditional agent, the Internet is much like the handheld computer organizer Jerry gave his father in an episode of *Seinfeld*. The elder Seinfeld was quite proud of what he kept calling his "tip calculator," ignorant of the device's many other sophisticated features and uses.

The corporate real estate website, though, is about as useful and dynamic as an actual tip calculator. Traditional agents try to promote its value because they don't have the volume, budget, or wherewithal to create and maintain powerful websites of their own. As I pointed out in chapter 2, the web developer is a vital member of my team, and having my own website is a key part of my marketing effort for sellers.

My personal website not only exposes my listings online, but it also allows me to target buyers in ways that agents relying on corporate websites can't. Buyers browsing properties on my site typically leave their names, phone numbers, and e-mail addresses when they see homes that interest them. I track, harvest, and analyze this data to create proprietary lists of buyers to whom I can market properties in very specific ways.

To give a basic example, if I'm marketing a home in neighborhood X, I can do a reverse search, and from the back end of my website, find everyone who browsed houses in that location. I then send them a message, since they left their e-mails when they registered, saying, "We have a new listing in neighborhood X and understand that you have been searching this area." Because they are usually either interested in buying there themselves or know someone who is, I achieve terrific results with this type of targeted marketing. Similarly, I can compile lists of people looking in particular price ranges for homes of a certain size or type.

Agents relying on corporate websites can't manipulate the data and get to buyers this way, because they don't control it. They don't have access to meaningful analytics. And again, even if they had their own websites, most agents wouldn't do enough volume to produce useful targeted lists. Agents touting cookie-cutter corporate sites never mention that they can't access the most important activity that occurs there. I compete with those sites but have the advantage of being fully in control of my own platform.

According to "The Digital House Hunt," a joint study by the National Association of Realtors® and Google, nine out of ten home buyers rely on the Internet as a primary research source, and most start their home searches online.[2] Is it important that your real estate agent has his or her own website, compiles targeted buyer lists, and understands how to market to the right buyers online? Absolutely. It's more important every day, and as an agent, I would find it difficult to justify the sizeable commissions that sellers pay me if I weren't supplying this kind of marketing muscle in return.

This isn't a book about marketing, however, so I'm only scratching the surface of my team's online strategies. Facebook, for instance, is an important part of my social media campaigns, and all of my listings show up as posts on my page. YouTube has become a popular real estate tool, and my team exposes homes there, too. We use Google, Yahoo, Bing, and Instagram; real estate sites like Trulia and Zillow; and too many other outlets to discuss here.

My goal in this chapter is simply to give you enough knowledge of online real estate marketing so that you are able to access how hard and how intelligently an agent will work to promote your home on the Internet. When you check out agents, ask about their personal website—if they even have one. Do they compile targeted buyer lists by mining data there? (If so, ask to see these lists and find out how they were compiled.) How do their personal websites—not the big brokerage ones—function on a mobile device? This is how many buyers now search, so the site that looks good on a laptop but not on a phone is problematic.

---

2   Jann Swanson, "Real Estate Web Searches Climb 253% in Four Years as 90% of Homebuyers Use Internet as Primary Research," January 7, 2013, Mortgage News Daily, http://www.mortgagenewsdaily.com/01072013_home_buying_behaviors.asp.

Ask the agents you're considering how they use big data online to target potential buyers and which platforms they're utilizing to reach them. Check out their social media profiles. If a prospective agent has only four listings in the last six months as posts on his or her Facebook page—or none—be wary. Go to Zillow, a very popular real estate site, and read the agent's reviews. Are they positive? How many are there? Buyers who aren't working with agents will call the ones who have had lots of reviews and listings on Zillow because they seem not only most successful, but they also appear to be the trusted local authority. Yet some consumers *still* hire agents who have very few sales or reviews on Zillow, which means they are hiring people who won't be answering questions on their home. If they're that disengaged, why hire them?

The Internet has become the most important marketing tool in a Realtor's® arsenal, yet many traditional agents don't take advantage of its full potential. I've focused on it for this reason, but I use many other types of marketing too, including print advertising, direct mail, radio, and TV. If, for instance, I've identified that target buyers for a particular property are sixty-plus, I realize that some of them don't spend much time online. I don't want to miss any potential buyers, so I might also use newspaper ads, postcards, and other means to reach them. Often, I use direct mail, too, to get neighbors to a launch. Many will show up out of simple curiosity, but other buyers don't know why they're browsing, and they add to the competitive environment I'm creating.

Building a competitive environment means reaching out to agents too. By doing reverse searches, my team assembles lists of agents who have sold homes in a particular area when we get a listing there. We let them know about our property, and they often have buyers who are interested.

All of these efforts are part of a strategy that's been developed and honed while selling hundreds upon hundreds of houses over many years. Frankly, I learned much of my approach the hard way, through trial and error. I've done enough research and development and spent enough money on things that didn't work to figure out what does. The agent selling four houses a year doesn't engage in this process. He can't invest in research and development, because he needs every dollar just to survive.

The list-and-pray approach to selling homes requires virtually no work—but effective, targeted marketing is quite labor intensive. Data must be collected and analyzed. Hundreds of prospecting calls must be made. Social media must be updated daily. The truth is, no single agent can do even a small part of what's required to reach the entire market. To give just one example, when I get a new listing, a full-time member of my team will contact every agent who sold a home during the last year in the same ZIP code. This is his job. Whatever promises an individual agent makes, he or she simply does not have the time to make those calls. If the agent actually does this, you should be even more worried because your listing is probably his only one. In that case, you have a hired a hobbyist, not a professional, to sell your home.

CHAPTER 8

PRICING YOUR HOME IN ANY MARKET

F or most agents, whether straight out of real estate school or thirty years in the business, pricing homes comes down to a single word: "comps." This, as you know if you've ever sold a home, stands for *comparables*, or *comparable properties*. Traditional agents, such as John or Jane, form their opinions about how a home should be priced by looking at the prices that several homes of a similar size, age, and style recently sold for in nearby locations. Find a few comparable properties, they think, and you've found the price a home should sell for.

At one time, coming up with comps and pricing homes were seen as a major part of the agent's job. Much of agents' value to sellers rested on access to the MLS, where they and they alone could search for comps. Those days are over, and as I've said elsewhere, if you're paying your sales agent for access to information, you would be better off attempting to market and sell a home yourself.

For starters, anyone can now go online and get data on recent sales in nearby locations—you no longer need an agent for that. More important, comps provide only one data point. A successful pricing strategy should take into account multiple data points, as well as presentation, in a thorough market positioning report—something which is exclusive to dynamic agents. My team looks at comps when pricing but also considers the concept of virtual shelf space, which we touched on in chapter 3. We analyze what's for sale and what's coming in the area, absorption rates, list-to-sales-price ratios, the average number of days homes are spending on market, and other factors.

We examine comps when planning our pricing strategy, but we would never rely only on them, partly because comps are old news. By definition, they indicate where the market was, past tense. We also want to factor in where the market is heading. To that end, we consider what's on market now and what's coming. Because we do such a high volume, we have a much better sense of this ebb and flow than the individual agent selling three or four homes a year.

Similarly, traditional agents think only in terms of price-per-square-foot. On its own, this metric can distort, since a home with high-end finishes will fetch a much higher price-per-square-foot than one with poor finishes next door. It can be one helpful measure, but the dynamic agent also considers the list-to-sales-price ratio in an area when positioning a home on market. This number, which expresses the difference in your listing price (what you put the home on the market for) and the actual sales price, can help us gauge where things are heading. An area's absorption rate, which measures how fast homes are coming on and off market, is another important indicator. How many days on average are homes being listed for, and is that number trending up or down? How are the local and national economies doing, and where do they appear to be heading? Are interest rates historically low or high, rising or falling?

Any agent can pull half a dozen comps and pick a price in the middle, but that's about as sophisticated as throwing a dart at a board covered in prices. Creating a market positioning report demands multiple data points and sophisticated analysis to determine an optimal list price. Most agents consider only a handful of comps, and few even understand the concept of virtual shelf space, to the detriment of the marketing effort.

Online, where most buyers begin browsing for homes, searches occur in brackets of $25,000, $50,000, and $100,000. Placing a home outside the appropriate bracket removes it from the search results that many target buyers will see. Home shoppers' eyes automatically go to the price bracket they want—just as in a store, consumers zoom in on the shelf with the wine or electronics in their range. A price that's strategically off by even $1,000 can hurt a home's online visibility by putting it on the wrong "virtual shelf," and agents who don't understand this component of pricing hurt sales every day.

Agents who work alone or with limited staff typically don't have the time or resources to tie all of the pertinent factors and data points together, along with presentation, to create a market positioning report. In fact, most have never heard of a market positioning report, though it's the best way to strategically market a home and gain a negotiating advantage over buyers. Sellers need to decide if they're willing to risk the sale of a massive asset on a "strategy" based on a handful of comps or if they want the kind of thorough strategy that will bring the greatest-possible market response.

Agents who close large volumes of homes—hundreds as opposed to three or four a year—have another inherent advantage when it comes to pricing. They have worked with enough buyers to know exactly what they want and value. If I have nearly identical houses, for example, but one has three bedrooms on a single level and the other has three bedrooms on multiple levels, I know that I have more buyers for the first house.

Now that I've introduced various factors involved in pricing, I'd like to broaden the discussion. Perhaps the most important point about pricing is this: When the marketing effort follows the sophisticated model I've presented in this book and gets sellers a full-market response, *the market determines the price.* That's right, the decision is made not by the seller, a Realtor®, or a single buyer, but by the entire market.

Think back to chapter 3 and the competitive sales environment I described, where buyers jockey against each other with an air of urgency, rather than with a seller. Done well, this sort of competitive sales strategy will result in full-market value for a home. The number might be slightly lower than the list price or it might be higher than the list price. The point is that in an auction-like environment, where buyers see each other's interest levels and feel competitive *with each other*, they will push the price to the most the market will bear, and often beyond it, since people hate to lose. This is a true full-market response, and in a real sense, the list price is nothing more than a guide.

If an agent knows how to get a full-market response—and very few do—in a way, it's impossible to underprice a home because the market will quickly correct that price. Here's a dramatic example. Let's say we took a $500,000 property and priced it at a dollar. We immediately would have a thousand people clamoring for the property. Hundreds of offers would come in, but the lowest ones would start to filter themselves out. Competing against each other, buyers would bid the price back up, and eventually, the true market price would emerge. Typically, the price goes over probable market value because people want to win.

Pricing aggressively brings buyers to a property and helps create the kind of full-market response I've been describing. Sellers frequently think, *If I want more for the house, I need to ask for more.* If the real estate market really worked that way, we could all start out by asking $10 million for every house. In reality, that sort of pricing drives buyers away, making a full-market response impossible. When you "premium price," you end up negotiating against one person who is not worried about losing the property to someone else. You push yourself up into the next value range, and the potential buyer compares your home to others that for slightly more money, offer more space, upgrades, amenities, etc.

There was a time when people visited even overpriced houses, with the expectation that they would negotiate prices down. Today, however, the first showing is on the Internet, and if you're overpriced, you won't get many buyers into your house. They are able to assess where you're at and examine the competition without leaving home. If they think you're overpriced online, they won't bother to show up and make that lowball offer.

THERE WAS A TIME WHEN PEOPLE VISITED EVEN OVERPRICED HOUSES, WITH THE EXPECTATION THAT THEY WOULD NEGOTIATE PRICES DOWN. TODAY, HOWEVER, THE FIRST SHOWING IS ON THE INTERNET, AND IF YOU'RE OVERPRICED, YOU WON'T GET MANY BUYERS INTO YOUR HOUSE.

Ironically, by keeping buyers away and preventing a competitive full-market response, holding out for a higher price results in a lower one. Remember, your power as a seller erodes a little more every day your home is still for sale, and the market is changing while you wait for that single, magical buyer to appear.

This results in a scenario we call "chasing the market." Before we discuss that in more depth, however, let's define a few terms. A buyers' market, as many of you probably know, means that the housing supply is greater than demand. High inventory gives buyers the advantage. A sellers' market is the opposite—demand is greater than supply, which means that sellers have the upper hand. A balanced market is in equilibrium, with supply and demand at similar levels.

In an "up," or sellers' market, it's harder to detect mistakes. The traditional agent who hasn't stoked competition might sell the home anyway, if the market is gaining, but a full-market response would have netted sellers perhaps 5 percent more. In this sort of environment, you don't truly know what your house is worth because you haven't tested the market. Even a skilled, dynamic agent doesn't fully know what the up market might bear, which is why it's vital to get the entire market to the property.

The seller might get the list price or very close to it, quickly, in an up market. But maybe, with a full-market response, multiple buyers in competition would have offered 5, 6, or 7 percent more. The homeowners are satisfied with the results because they don't know that there is a better method out there, a proven process that can exploit a sellers' market. They were happy to sell their house quickly, not knowing they might have left perhaps $50,000, or even much more, on the table.

Now let's return to the idea of "chasing the market," which can be a major roadblock for sellers in a "down" market. As I mentioned, in the down or buyers' market, inventory accumulates, with more and more homes up for sale. Homes that might have sold in a short amount of time six months ago linger. Price reductions become common. Buyers have a lot to choose from.

In this scenario, similar homes cluster around a price point. In a particular neighborhood, there might be many similar homes priced around $600,000, for example. Buyers in this scenario feel no urgency because those homes don't appear to be moving, and none are differentiating themselves. No one is showing greater value. Eventually, though, one of those sellers thinks, *I really need to sell because I have another house and a job waiting in Kansas. I have to get my family moved.* This seller adjusts the price down, moves the house out of the pricing cluster, and sells it.

The other sellers think, *Hmm, the Joneses just sold for $590,000. That's where the market is.* Over the course of weeks, they all start moving their price in line with that last sale and the Joneses' price. Well, now they're all clustered once again, and again, the buyer isn't seeing any differentiated value. The buyer, as before, feels no urgency. The cycle repeats, and eventually, one seller will price a house down out of the cluster. It will sell, and the other homes again will follow to that price point—perhaps $580,000 this time.

This is "chasing the market." The seller is always moving to where the last sale was, and so are all the other sellers—repositioning themselves multiple times while the market slides. In a down market, it's critical to price intelligently in order to get out in front of that pattern. You want to be the next to sell so that you're the highest step on that ladder. You want to get just ahead of the market as a *new* listing, when you're more likely to have multiple buyers expressing interest together, a scenario that gives you more negotiating leverage. You want to sell quickly, without having to reposition, perhaps over and over, while the market slides and your power as a buyer erodes because of growing market time.

Sellers frequently want to ignore market time. They say they're in no hurry to sell, they just want the best price for their home, as if marketing a home patiently month after month eventually will achieve a higher price. This isn't the case. In fact, the longer a house sits on the market, the more aggressive buyers will get with their offers. Pricing history is publicly available online and buyers use it as leverage. *The house has been sitting here forever,* buyers think. *I can go in lower because nobody else has been interested.* In fact, selling for the most you can is the same as selling a home as quickly as you can, if you're creating a competitive environment and getting a full-market response.

Sellers often wonder, too, if they should get an appraisal as they're preparing to price a home for sale. The appraisal system is complex, but suffice it to say that, first of all, an appraisal is simply one person's opinion, not a full-market valuation. The appraiser spends perhaps an hour on a property, which might be in a neighborhood he or she has never even visited before. An appraisal does *not* necessarily represent market value.

The other thing to keep in mind is that the buyers' lenders will order their own appraisal from a third party and use that number to write the loan, so an appraisal from the seller becomes irrelevant. The lender's appraisal can come in below the buyers' offer sometimes, in which case it's more important than ever to have a dynamic agent in your corner. A buyer who has made an offer out of the kind of competitive environment we create is more likely to meet the seller halfway if an appraisal comes in low and add cash of his or her own to the loan amount, knowing that if he or she doesn't, another buyer will. The buyer who offers $500,000 and then sees a bank appraisal pegging the value at $450,000 is often willing to add $25,000 or more out of pocket to make the deal work, knowing the seller had multiple offers.

A similar situation can arise with home inspections, a standard part of the sales process these days. Again, if buyers have made their offer after seeing the interest of other buyers in a competitive environment, they're less likely to insist on renegotiating because of problems a home inspector discovered.

I'll finish this chapter with the story of a home inspection that turned up a significant issue at a house I sold a while back. I had created a competitive environment and had two offers on the property, both at full price. The sellers chose the first one, but the buyer's home inspector said that the big wraparound deck on this waterfront house was not in good shape. It would cost $25,000 to replace.

I told the buyer's specialist to send me the report, but pointed out that my sellers might not be willing to renegotiate, since they had another full-price offer on the table. The buyers relented the next day and, afraid that they might lose the house to competitors, didn't ask for a penny out of that $25,000.

CHAPTER 9

DOES YOUR AGENT HAVE YOUR BEST INTERESTS IN MIND?

When you're selling a home, your real estate agent works for you, so it would be reasonable to assume that he or she has your best interests in mind. It would also be reasonable to assume that your interests and the agent's interests are one and the same. Reasonable thinking—but not always accurate. Far too many traditional agents don't have the consumer's best interests in mind when they take listings, market properties, or work with buyers. Unfortunately, agents who are unscrupulous, desperate, or both often use customers for their own ends, to the detriment of the deal.

One common unscrupulous practice involves agents willingly taking on overpriced listings. They go along with whatever number the seller wants to hear, even though they know from glancing at comparable properties that they can't get that price for the home. This keeps the seller happy in the short term but causes a world of pain in the long term. Today's buyers are savvy, and as they react to the high price, the agent who raised no objections at listing time inevitably will hit the sellers with price reductions as the months drag on.

Overpricing a property and then letting it stagnate or reducing the price repeatedly over weeks and months completely undercuts the seller's position. As I've emphasized elsewhere, every day that a house sits on market erodes the power of the seller. The agent knows this, and knew when listing the home that it probably couldn't appraise for such a steep price, but he or she took the listing anyway.

Why? Well, the overpriced listing will take forever to sell and ultimately come in at a much lower price than if it was assessed correctly to begin with, but in some ways, traditional agents can benefit even if a home never sells. Their signs sit in yards advertising their names and phone numbers. Some look at this as essentially a free billboard. The longer the sign is up, the more exposure they get.

Neighbors see these signs and call such agents about selling their own homes. Passing drivers see the signs, call, and inquire about the properties. They might not be interested in buying a particular home once they find out it's overpriced, but unethical agents can add the potential buyers to their database and sell them other properties. Endless open houses at overpriced homes become a burden for sellers as weeks stretch into months and the Realtor® becomes a weekend fixture at the house, but those events produce more leads for agents. The overpriced listing, so bad for sellers, becomes a lead magnet in the hands of agents who sell so few homes they'll take whatever comes along.

My team of dynamic agents and I obviously want to sell a home for the maximum price we can. It's good for our clients and good for us—the higher the sales price, the more money we make. We work tirelessly to create a competitive environment and a full-market response in order to get the maximum price the market will bear, but we also try to set realistic expectations on listing appointments. An overpriced home makes a full-market response impossible because it keeps potential buyers away and ultimately results in less, not more, money for a home. Occasionally, we meet with a seller who insists on sticking to an exorbitant price that's out of line with our market positioning report, and I politely decline to take the listing. Putting a home on the market at a price that will keep buyers away is only going to hurt the seller in the long term, and I don't want to hurt my own client. As we'll discuss in chapter 12, this is why it's important to find an agent with a track record of selling homes quickly and learn how close to the asking price he or she sells on average.

Agents who work alone and sell a handful of homes each year offer inferior service in other ways too. For example, the same person will represent buyers and sellers in a single transaction. Our team has buyer specialists (covered in chapter 10), so if we wind up representing both parties in a transaction, there typically is one designated person with an assigned role looking out for the seller's interests and another for the buyer's. They don't share information in this scenario, conducting their business as if they were in different offices. This guarantees a high level of expertise, service, and professionalism. The team approach helps ensure that your agent is looking out for you, not using you.

As I've emphasized throughout this book, sellers entrust what for many is their greatest asset in a real estate agent's hands. It's vital that this person is honest with his or her clients, but honesty can be difficult when dealing with a home. It might be hard to hear that some aspect of a house your family has treasured for decades will hurt the sales effort if it isn't changed or fixed, but a dynamic, ethical agent will deliver those hard truths.

Sellers might agree that, say, the carpeting is ratty and needs to be replaced, but as I mentioned in chapter 6, they often prefer to give a $2,000 credit to buyers rather than tear up the living room. It's the job of a conscientious, professional agent to explain that spending $2,000 to replace the carpet now will get the sellers full-market value from the improvement and potentially save them far more money down the road. Why? Well, buyers inevitably think new carpeting will cost twice the actual amount, and many will avoid the house altogether because they're put off by the unsightly flooring. Fewer buyers showing up chips away at the competitive environment and price. In the end, an agent who avoids a difficult conversation for his or her own comfort dumps the listing in the MLS as is and turns that $2,000 improvement into a $6,000 loss.

Because they lack experience and sales volume, some agents don't know the best steps sellers should take to prepare any given home for sale. Others may have ideas on what's needed, but because they're selling three or five homes in a good year, they're afraid to have those tough conversations. They don't have much experience with such talks, and they can't afford to risk losing a commission.

It's not that Jane Smith, the average traditional agent, is by nature a devious or unethical person. But Jane is struggling to survive, working just to put gas in the car and food on the table, and her desperation can lead to poor service and representations that are less than honest. Having her own website would allow her to premarket a property as "coming soon" and to collect leads online. But Jane can't afford to build or maintain her own website, so she touts the big brokerage website, which she can't control or leverage for sellers in any meaningful way.

Similarly, brother John Smith might talk about his "marketing plan" or "marketing program," but the truth is that the corporate website, a yard sign, and the MLS comprise nearly all the tools in his arsenal. We, by contrast, take a sophisticated multipronged approach to marketing that includes online advertising, social media, print advertising, calls to potential buyers, and more. Are John and Jane serving their clients' best interests by skipping all these steps in favor of a "list-and-pray" approach? Of course not—it's an incredibly risky way to market a vital asset—but the seller assumes all of the risk, and the Smith siblings don't have another option.

Traditional agents who take overpriced listings, use sellers simply to advertise their own business, and misrepresent their marketing strategies aren't helping their clients, and because they essentially work alone, they couldn't do an adequate job even with the best intentions. The dynamic agent, with an entire team behind him or her, is much better positioned to serve sellers every step of the way.

CHAPTER 10

PUT A BUYER SPECIALIST IN YOUR CORNER

I hope by now readers understand that all Realtors® are not created equal and that it's important to choose an experienced professional who can demonstrate a proven process to sell your home. This is so important that I'll devote all of chapter 12 to the things you should look for when selecting a sales agent. It is equally important, however, to find an experienced *buyer specialist* when you decide to purchase a home.

The topic can be a murky one because many consumers don't even know that there's a difference between a *listing specialist*, who is focused on sales, and a *buyer specialist*, who looks out for the buyers' interests, negotiates on their behalf, and provides an edge when it's time to make a deal.

When a buyer begins shopping for property, he or she will often call an agent who sold a previous home for them, or for friends or neighbors. This person—it could be one of our old friends John or

Jane, if they got lucky and closed one of those four annual deals next door—will happily show up and drive the buyer around to look at houses. The agent will probably start with his or her own listings, if there are any in the buyer's preferred area and price range, but will also broaden the search to homes listed by other agents. John or Jane will discuss pricing and locations and specifics about these various houses and a host of pluses and minuses with the buyer. After a couple of weeks of this, the buyer will get used to this and be glad that someone's looking out for his or her interests.

Except that someone *isn't*.

Listing specialists work for home *sellers*, not the buyers in a transaction.

Many buyers, understandably, are unclear on this point and don't see that taking advice from John or Jane on a deal is sort of like asking the prosecutor to make your closing arguments when you're on trial. Would you ever go to court without your own attorney? Of course not, so why would you purchase an asset worth hundreds of thousands, if not millions, of dollars without representation? Buyers need someone in their corner, fighting for them, just as much as sellers do.

People's first reaction to the idea of a buyer specialist is often that it sounds good—but what's the cost? That's a great question, and the answer—virtually nothing—is the biggest reason that buyers should work with a buyer specialist. In most real estate deals, the listing specialist splits the commission with a cooperating agent. The split is the same whether that agent is another listing specialist who happened to bring buyers to a showing or a buyer specialist truly working for the buyers. In both scenarios, the home seller pays the commission. This means that using a buyer specialist, someone who's legally and ethically bound to look out for the buyers' sole benefit and interest, is essentially free. There is no downside to using a buyer specialist.

There are, however, lots of upsides. In chapter 2, "It Takes a Team," I pointed out the importance of specialization. The individual agent who attempts to wear all necessary hats—doing his or her own marketing, photographing properties, answering calls, showing homes, shepherding contracts to closing, etc.—simply can't do a good job. That's why my team has experts devoted to various parts of the process. One of the most important members of our team is the buyer specialist, who spends all day every day working with buyers and, apart from being legally bound to protect their interests, is attuned to their needs.

As a buyer, do you want a listing specialist, who works for sellers, advising you on a purchase, or do you want an expert who works for *you* negotiating your end of the deal? You don't go to a general practitioner for heart surgery. If you have cancer, you'd likely go to a particular kind of specialist depending on whether it's lung or prostate cancer. When you hire an attorney, is it for a case involving tax law, litigation, or contracts? The need determines the professional you choose, and real estate is no different. To randomly pick a generalist who doesn't even work for your interests makes little sense. The person who did a great job selling your last house might be second-rate when it comes to buying your next one.

Even many consumers who have heard of buyer's specialists don't use them, thinking they can save money by not hiring one. There's a common misconception that having a single agent handle a transaction somehow saves on commission or results in a lower price. This simply isn't true—and in fact, not using a buyer specialist tends to cost buyers significant money. The commission is set with the seller early in the process and, as I've explained, won't change whether the agent who brings a buyer to the table is another listing specialist or a buyer specialist. Having one agent handle the entire deal doesn't save a cent. It just means you're going through an important high-dollar deal without representation.

Obviously, having the opposing party's counsel represent you in a lawsuit wouldn't help when it came time for a judgment. Similarly, buyers never know how much better they might have done in a transaction had they used a buyer specialist, but the odds are good that they could have gotten a better price, better terms, or at least, sounder sleep. A buyer specialist—a seasoned expert scrutinizing every aspect of a deal—might save buyers thousands on the sales price and certainly provides peace of mind.

Another advantage to using a buyer specialist is the access to off-market homes and "hidden inventory" that he or she can give you. If, as a buyer, you simply visit advertised open houses and check out the next home on Zillow or the next property sent from your agent's automated online search, then you're chasing the same homes as everyone else, and the good ones tend to go fast. The deals get snapped up, and you're always a step behind. Buyer specialists will not only get you in front of those homes as soon as possible, but they also can unlock hidden inventory.

Buyer specialists have one function in the business—matching buyers with homes. They're not worried about recruiting and hiring, finances, marketing, etc. They focus all their energy on their dedicated buyer clients, which means they can sit down, map out exactly what their buyers are looking for, and dig it up.

Having access to a team's "coming-soon" listings before they're in the MLS, but prospecting in the area you like, buyer specialists also turn up other properties that aren't on the market yet but soon will be. They explore neighborhoods you are interested in, knock on doors, call old expired listings that never sold, call homes that are currently for rent to see if the owners will sell, and use other high-value methods to create inventory. This is the real magic of a strong buyer specialist.

Buyer specialists use their expertise to take care of buyers in other ways too. They're not salespeople so much as consultants who absorb buyers' wants, tastes, and needs and then direct them to the properties that are going to meet those criteria. This is key because what buyers think they want in a home when they start searching and what they later decide to buy are almost always two different things. Oftentimes, after shopping with their clients for a while, buyer specialists come to know what buyers want better than the buyers do themselves. For instance, buyers might tell me that they want a three-bedroom, two-bathroom house. They keep browsing homes with two bedrooms upstairs and one down but not liking any of them. I soon realize that we need to cull the list to houses with three bedrooms on one level. This is what they actually want—and while they're wasting time looking for other layouts, they might lose out on the perfect home.

My buyer specialists are continually listening to buyers' reactions, noting what they say they like and don't like, and looking out for quiet cues, too (i.e., the things they happily linger over or hesitate on.) Buyers sometimes can't express or don't fully understand their own hang-ups and preferences, but it's part of the buyer specialist's job to collect the clues, consult, and make appropriate suggestions. In this regard, a buyer's specialist can save significant time as well as money and make the process much easier for both buyers and sellers. For instance, my team helped a couple that was adamant they need over two thousand finished square feet and wouldn't look at anything that was smaller than that. But what they were getting in their price range was older when they got up to that size of a home, and the floor plans were more compartmentalized. In the end, we ended up selling them a 1,600 finished square foot newer home that had the vaulted ceilings and an open floor plan. Even though the home did not meet their initial size criteria, it wasn't really the size that was the issue. It was the big open spaces they were missing, which they were able to find in a newer (but smaller) home that actually felt larger.

To be honest, there's an element of marriage counselor in being a buyer's specialist too. A husband and wife shopping for a home are not always going to be on the same page. Buyer specialists try to find the middle ground. Maybe *he* wants a big garage and *she* would like a gourmet kitchen. Well, the buyer's specialist might highlight that a particular listing with an amazing kitchen has only an average garage but includes a huge storage shed out back. The buyers might have skipped that otherwise-perfect house, noting the two-car garage, but a little digging by the buyer specialist reveals that they can both have what they want there.

Some first-time buyers want everything shiny but have trouble seeing beyond the surface. A home that an investor flipped might have great new floors and stainless-steel appliances and look pretty at first glance. That's fine, but perhaps the buyers aren't noticing that the windows are rotted and the roof shingles are curling and the siding is ancient. Despite its fresh gloss, the house is far from maintenance-free.

It's the job of the buyer's specialist to make sure those buyers are educated. They might still want the property, but they need to know that the windows, roof, and siding need work—and that these are big-ticket items. They should also know that, realistically, they won't get much value from those repairs when they go to sell because their buyers will expect those items to be in good working order already.

Rehabbers know exactly what they're doing when they add fresh paint, carpeting, and stainless-steel appliances to catch buyers' eyes. Buyer specialists get their clients to see the *entire* property, warts and all. This can be challenging even with discerning, experienced buyers when they feel an instant emotional attachment to a house.

The location is perfect, and the kitchen looks stunning with those granite counters and stainless steel appliances. Great, but what about the impending roof replacement and rotting siding? The buyer specialist can point out that a house one block away has the same sterling location and though less glossy, is solid, with a good roof, updated siding, and no significant deferred maintenance. Investing in stainless-steel appliances and granite counters and refinishing the floors will make it look every bit as good as the other option, but for much less money in the long run. This is the kind of math a good buyer's specialist can do for his or her clients—helping them to think strategically.

Similarly, buyers might be interested in suburb X but not find anything they like in their price range. The buyer's specialist can point out that homes in adjacent neighborhood Y are priced more affordably and just six blocks away. Why waste time in a location that doesn't have what you want when there's a terrific nearby equivalent option?

Because buyer specialists save their clients enormous amounts of time, it's a good idea to contact one as soon as you think you're going to buy or begin browsing homes online. If you're dealing with a lawsuit, you don't meet your attorney in the courtroom. You meet him or her at the office, have a consultation, put together a game plan, and know in advance exactly where you're going. It's the same with buying a home, or should be. An initial half-hour consultation with a buyer's specialist typically will save you days of chasing the wrong things, unclear about what you're going after or what's out there. When they don't go about the search in targeted ways, buyers can waste hours perusing homes that don't meet their requirements.

Consult with a buyer's specialist as early as you can, even months before you're ready to look. When you're buying a home, you have conversations about the process with your spouse, friends, and coworkers. It's a big deal and consumes energy even before you start visiting properties. Many buyers spend that energy, over months and months, on all the wrong things—a price point they won't actually buy in, locations that turn out to be wrong, features they'll forego. They avoid talking to an agent because they're months from being able to purchase, but that's exactly when they should consult a professional. Such a consultation will make those months of discussing and preparing worthwhile. They'll be targeted. Buyers will think and discuss more clearly and plan strategically instead of being unfocused or unrealistic.

One of the first things buyer specialists do is have their clients talk to a lender, if they haven't already, and assist with getting mortgage preapproval. Once buyers take that step, their specialist can talk to them about what their price point should be, based on what they want to spend. This will, of course, depend on the kind of loan they can get, the down-payment requirements, current interest rates, and more.

Sometimes buyers are frustrated by not being able to find homes with enough space or certain features, and the buyer's specialist can point out that they're unnecessarily restricting themselves to a particular price point, when in reality, they can afford a higher one where the house they want actually exists. Other times, buyers begin their searches looking at homes they can't afford, either because they won't get approval for the necessary mortgage or because they can get approved but will then face too high a monthly payment. The formula is complex, affected by the loan amount buyers are approved for, the size of their down payment, the monthly payment they feel comfortable making, and ever-fluctuating interest rates. An early consultation with a buyer specialist can make all this clearer and streamline the home-buying process—and regular coaching along the way can be invaluable too. For instance, a buyer's specialist might highlight for clients that recent downticks in interest rates mean they now can afford a higher price point for the same monthly payment than when they first did the math.

I'll conclude this chapter by emphasizing once again that it makes no sense to enter into something as important as a home purchase without representation, especially when using the services of a buyer specialist is essentially free. Ideally, the person you hire should be part of an experienced team with a proven track record. The prettiest girl doesn't stay single long, and the best houses at the best prices don't linger on the market either. As a buyer, you can't afford to miss a single opportunity, and definitely not because the agent you're working with was distracted by answering random phone calls, keeping a listing appointment, reviewing ads, or any of fifty other tasks.

A team that does significant volume has specialists for all of those tasks, so buyer's specialists can focus. The professional team also offers expert coverage at all times so that if a particular buyer specialist is occupied, the buyer won't miss out on a hot property or lose a single opportunity.

CHAPTER 11

BUSTING REAL ESTATE MYTHS

The real estate industry is full of myths, misinformation, and faulty wisdom. Traditional agents who haven't changed with the times like it this way, and they often work to keep the myths alive. They rely on outdated beliefs to get customers and then attempt to sell houses using outdated methods. In many cases, there's nothing duplicitous about this. Old-school agents like our friends John and Jane Smith frequently believe in the myths as firmly as home sellers.

The problem with relying on myths in real estate is that they can cost homeowners enormous amounts of time and many thousands of dollars—sometimes even six figures or more—when they sell. In this chapter, I'll tackle the most common myths and misperceptions about selling homes, and in the next, I'll provide a checklist of the concrete for in order to select a dynamic agent who isn't decades behind the times. If you take nothing else from this book, these two chapters alone provide, I hope, an invaluable guide to finding the right agent and navigating the sales process.

I could probably fill an entire book with real estate myths, but here are some of the most common.

MYTH #1—REAL ESTATE AGENTS ARE ALL THE SAME.

The myth that all agents are the same is perhaps the most expensive one out there. Think back to the early chapters of this book. There is a massive difference between the quality of service and professionalism a team of experts delivers compared to that of a single agent attempting to wear all the hats necessary in this complex process. Remember the thorough strategy I presented for creating a competitive sales environment and a full-market response in chapter 3? It's far different from the kind of "list-and-pray" approach many traditional agents offer. Compare the effort a professional team puts into market positioning, top-notch photography, staging, and marketing with Jane Smith's effort, sticking a sign in the yard and snapping a few pics for her corporate website.

I won't belabor it here, but one of my main arguments in the book has been that all agents are not created equal. A related myth is that just because agents work for the same brokerage, this doesn't mean they offer the same level of service. Real estate agents are independent operators. Within the same big brokerage office, each agent creates his or her own strategy and marketing budget. One might have her own website, while another relies on the ineffective corporate site. One might take a sophisticated approach to marketing homes on multiple social media platforms, while another puts up a single Facebook post for each new listing. One might have an entire team, while another works alone.

The process—or lack thereof—varies widely from one agent to the next and from one team to the next. Keep the checklist I'll provide in chapter 12 handy and interview multiple agents to see exactly what your money will buy when you hire one.

MYTH #2—HIRE THE NEIGHBORHOOD EXPERT.

Having an agent with community knowledge doesn't hurt, but frankly, it's less important in the Internet age. When information was harder to access, consumers valued real estate agents' knowledge of local schools, hospitals, restaurants, etc. Today, this information is widely available online, where we can read reviews and easily compare crime rates and school test scores—and even walk down virtual streets. The best and most current neighborhood information no longer comes from real estate agents.

What you need, instead, is an agent who can activate a full-market response, which means reaching potential buyers from all over, not just the immediate community. The odds are good that potential buyers in the surrounding neighborhood will find out about your home, from word of mouth, another agent, or a yard sign. But very few homes sell to a nearby buyer, and the agent who's too focused on one area will miss most of your potential market. If your agent is a local celebrity when it comes to the neighborhood, that's great, but the new neighborhood is really the *Internet*—and that's where the home-buying process begins. If your agent doesn't know *that* neighborhood intimately—and most traditional agents don't—few buyers show up and a full-market response becomes impossible.

MYTH #3—ALWAYS SELL AFTER
THE SUPER BOWL.

This myth is common not only in places like Minnesota, with bone-chilling winters, but also in mild climates like San Diego's. Consumers simply think "winter"—whatever that means wherever they live—is a bad time to sell a house. First of all, the optimal time to sell is when inventory is low (supply is down), and that can fluctuate regardless of the season. Second, because of the winter myth, we do see an increase in the number of buyers in spring and summer, but we also see a massive increase in inventory. Sellers who go to market in winter might have a smaller pool of buyers, but they also have much less competition.

Buyers who are in the market during winter months tend to be more serious and feel more urgency about purchasing. Often, they are relocating for work, just had a baby, got divorced, etc. A life change means they want to buy as quickly as possible, which puts the seller in a good position. The spring season, by contrast, is when the "tire-kickers" come out. It's still a good time to sell because more buyers come into the market, but a higher percentage of them are hobbyists and window-shoppers.

Wherever you live, remember that much of the home-buying process now occurs online. On laptops, consumers can search as easily for homes in unpleasant weather or during the holidays as they can during pleasanter months. The bottom line: Put your home on the market when you feel ready to. If you'd like to sell your home and move to Texas in November, don't put your life on hold for four months, waiting for "buying season." There's no such thing anymore.

MYTH #4—THE AGENT PRICES YOUR HOME.

Many sellers think price is the first and final word in the selling process. They believe that pricing a home correctly is *the* key to selling it, and that finding some magic number is the Realtor's® main job. Nothing could be further from the truth, and as I've said elsewhere, if pricing is the biggest thing your agent brings to the table, you might as well sell the home yourself.

You need an agent—actually, an entire team—who can deliver a full-market response. When you bring the entire market to the home and create a competitive environment, ultimately, the market will price the house. I covered pricing thoroughly in chapter 8, so I'll just touch on the pricing myth here, but the key point is that developing a market positioning report and arriving at a list price right for the market is only a part of the process. The important thing in this stage is to make sure that a home is not priced in such a way that it keeps buyers from showing up or keeps the house from appearing in the appropriate brackets in online search results.

If your team does a strategic analysis and gets your home in the right "virtual shelf space" (covered in chapter 8), the most important part of the pricing process then becomes producing a full-market response. That means multiple buyers feeling urgency in a competitive environment that will, through multiple offers, get the price to its market value—and often (because no one likes to lose) beyond it.

MYTH #5—SUCCESSFUL AGENTS UNDERPRICE HOMES.

Traditional agents who sell three or four homes a year are none too happy when a dynamic agent in his or her market is selling homes by the dozens or even hundreds. A common snipe leveled against successful agents is that they produce high volume by underpricing homes.

Such outdated agents might have this in mind when sellers interview them to decide who should list their home. In fact, they might even aim high when telling sellers where they would price their home, knowing that some homeowners might interview three agents and lean toward the one who names the highest list price. An agent like that might suggest $403,000 for a house his or her competitor argues should list for $399,000.

It's understandable that some sellers gravitate toward the higher price, but it's quite possible that the slightly lower list price in this example will result in a higher sales price. The traditional agent has priced the sellers out of the appropriate bracket in online-search results for the sake of getting the listing (I discussed the importance of these brackets in chapters 3 and 8). Now, buyers stay away, the home languishes on the market, and eventually, the price gets reduced, possibly several times—possibly to a number well below $399,000.

If John's competitor is a dynamic agent, his or her full-market response might well result in a price higher than $403,000—no one knows for sure until motivated buyers are pitted against each other in a competitive environment. But with one traditional agent who doesn't know how to harness the market, sellers never know if they achieved full-market value.

MYTH #6—HIRE THE AGENT WITH THE LOWEST COMMISSION.

The shoddy logic behind this myth is apparent. Sure, commission is important, but comparing commissions in a vacuum is a little like saying, "Pay $30,000 for your next car." If I'm buying a brand new

Bentley, that's the steal of the century, but if it's a used 1980 Kia, I'm getting ripped off.

Commission is meaningless until you know what it buys you. If you take nothing else from this book, think about home selling—and question sales agents—in terms of *process*. A full-service commission with the right team might be an incredible bargain because they will net you more money for your home in less time. A discounted commission with a traditional agent who works alone, taking a list-and-pray approach, might be far too much, considering what you get. What are you receiving for the commission you pay? What is the agent's process? These are vital questions, and I'll give you the concrete tools to answer them in the next chapter.

CHAPTER 12

HIRING AN AGENT: THE INSIDER'S CHECKLIST

I've given you lots of information about the ways that the real estate industry is broken and why many traditional agents don't do much to earn the significant commissions that sellers pay them. But what's a homeowner to do? In this chapter—perhaps the most important in the book—I'll give you a checklist to use when hiring an agent. American consumers have gotten savvier about choosing many kinds of professionals, from contractors to doctors, thanks in part to the Internet. You can use similar online-review tools to find dynamic agents whose promise to get the most the market can bear for your home in the shortest time is not idle.

I'll point you toward some of those tools here and provide others, so that consumers know exactly what questions to ask prospective agents and how to compare them using meaningful metrics. Let me say again that all agents are not created equal. I recommend that you interview several, analyze their track records, and find out what *process* each can deliver. It doesn't hurt that your neighbor or cousin recommended an agent, but don't rely on their judgment. Many thousands of dollars and months of frustration could hang in the balance.

A PERSONAL CUSTOM WEBSITE

Before you even bother to interview an agent, ask for his or her individual website's URL—not the address of the big corporate website but the one the agent had custom-made for his or her own business. These big company websites are good sites and do serve a purpose, but that purpose doesn't necessarily help out sellers. As I've explained elsewhere, individual agents don't have control of such sites or access to the analytics and data needed for thorough online prospecting. Hiring an agent without his or her own website is like hiring a taxi driver without a taxi. He might be a decent driver, but he's missing a key tool necessary to get you where you need to go.

Company-controlled websites get their agents' listings when they're entered in the MLS. By then, the clock is ticking and the seller is accumulating days on market. Agents must have their own custom websites, which they build and control, in order to do premarket promotion, so vital in any sales effort. The agent also needs to be able to collect data on all potential buyers who are browsing his or her site, and that isn't possible with the corporate sites.

The agent's personal site should look professional. Find out how much traffic it gets, and see how it does in Internet search results. Ask the agent for the official rankings, but also test this yourself by doing Google searches and seeing where, or if, the agent's site appears in results.

GOOD ZILLOW / TRULIA PROFILES

Go to these popular real estate websites and check out the reviews of prospective agents. This is a quick, easy way not only to see what consumers have to say about agents but also to check on how many homes they have sold in the last year and how many times they've been reviewed. You can see an agent's active listings, recent sales, areas of expertise, and more. Someone who's getting few reviews, or bad ones, or is doing fewer than one hundred sales annually shouldn't be trusted to sell your home. This is a good way to weed out agents before you even pick up the phone.

A STRONG LIST-TO-SALES-PRICE RATIO

As I pointed out in the last chapter, commissions can't be compared unless you also have a way to compare the value they buy you. Looking at what we call the "list-to-sales-price ratio" allows you to compare apples to apples. This number simply represents the on-average percentage of the list price that an agent gets at closing. An agent with a ratio of 95 percent is likely to get $475,000 for a house he or she lists at $500,000 ($475,000 is 95 percent of $500,000).

Commission matters, but if the average agent is getting 95 percent of listed sales price, and another team is averaging 100 percent, even if the second team's commission is 1 percent more, the seller will make 4 percent more money at the end of the day. Make prospective agents document this important ratio with official printouts from the MLS.

AVERAGE DAYS ON MARKET

Like the list-to-sales-price ratio, the average number of days an agent's listings spend on the market is an important tool for comparison. If one agent's average time on the market is more than a year and another's is forty days, that's important to know. Lengthy average-market time might be a sign that the agent is taking overpriced listings or that he or she is incompetent, or both. Most sellers want to measure their sales time in weeks, not years, and for good reason. Their overall finances are hurt by having to carry a home longer than anticipated—paying for insurance, maintenance, taxes, etc.— and longer market times result in lower sales prices. Buyers expect a deal when they notice a home lingering on the market month after month. This is the exact opposite of the full-market response and sense of urgency that leads to a successful sale.

A HEALTHY MARKETING BUDGET

Finding out what your agent spends on marketing also will help you compare commissions and levels of service. My team spends an enormous amount of money and resources on marketing. Because we do a large volume, we can afford to make a little less on each home we sell and plow a significant portion of commissions into marketing. Traditional agents selling four houses a year often have no real marketing budget. Because they see so few commissions, they need every cent for themselves.

SIZEABLE DATABASES

The individual agent selling a few houses a year probably has a pretty short list of leads. Find out how big agents' databases of leads are in concrete terms. How heavy is traffic on their custom websites, and how many leads are they harvesting there? How many buyers registered on their website last year? How many followers do they have on Facebook and other social media platforms? How long is their list of agents who potentially have clients interested in your home?

NO "HOSTAGE AGREEMENTS"

Some agents, especially old-school ones who are afraid of losing listings that linger on market, convince sellers to sign contracts that bind them for six months. A dissatisfied seller is then stuck with an agent he or she doesn't want. Even without such a defined term, listing agreements in most states tend to be friendlier to agents than to consumers. Insist on an agreement that guarantees, in writing, that you can stop working with an agent at any time for any reason without penalty. If that's not included right up front, then the agent is not looking out for you—but, rather, him or herself.

AN EXPERT TEAM

Do agents work alone, or perhaps with a single assistant, or do they have an entire team working on the sales effort? As we explored in chapter 2, the agent who tries to wear all the necessary hats offers poor service, more or less relying on prayer and yard signs to sell homes. Getting a full-market response requires a listing specialist, a marketing coordinator, an operations manager, a runner, and more. A good team uses a professional photographer and stager. Without the right experts and support staff, the marketing effort is doomed.

A DOCUMENTED MARKETING PLAN

Do the agents you're considering have marketing plans that they can detail during an appointment at your home? What are the various prongs of their marketing effort? How exactly will they use their own website and social media platforms to leverage leads? Where and how do they advertise? How do they use photography, videos, mailers, radio, or TV ads? Does their marketing plan include exposure before a home is in the MLS, with a "coming-soon" program, or do they wait until it's in the system and accumulating days on market?

ALL-INCLUSIVE SERVICE

My team's commission includes a sophisticated marketing strategy with many elements—all included in the price. Other agents might talk about some of those elements, but do they charge extra for them? Watch out for hidden fees later when it comes to photography, staging, online advertising, etc.

A MARKET POSITIONING REPORT

Are agents glancing at a few comparable properties quickly printed from the MLS, or are they providing a thorough market positioning report? In addition to comparable properties, market positioning reports also consider the concept of virtual shelf space, which we touched on in chapter 3. They analyze what's for sale and what's coming in an area, absorption rates, list-to-sales-price ratios, the average number of days homes are spending on market, and other factors.

AN EQUITY EVALUATION

The right agent will provide sellers with an equity evaluation. This analysis of how much equity sellers have in their home is important in strategizing and setting expectations for a sale.

PROFESSIONAL PHOTOGRAPHY

This is a must in the age of online marketing. As I've pointed out, you have a matter of seconds to grab buyers' attention online and interrupt their automatically clicking onto the next photo. We win with presentation every time because we use top professional photographers. They are trained and experienced in architectural photography, a distinct art with unique challenges. Lighting a home correctly and capturing its spaces in the ways that will show best online is a complex process. Agents taking their own photos or using some kid from the office rarely get it right and should not be trusted to market your home.

A VIDEO-MARKETING PLAN

Today's buyers don't just want to see photos of homes, they want to watch videos of them. Having a video can separate you from sellers who don't. Check with prospective agents to see how they use video marketing and live streaming, such as Facebook Live.

A CALL-CAPTURE SYSTEM

All professional agents should have a *call-capture* system that records every incoming number and call, so that they are permanently stored in the system for follow-up. Every lead for every single seller is precious. Do not hire an agent who simply has calls going to his or her voicemail, or worse, the brokerage office secretary, who might or might not pass them on quickly. My team tracks every call, to determine where each came from and which marketing methods are working for our clients.

AT LEAST FOUR HUNDRED ANNUAL SALES

If agents haven't sold at least four hundred homes in the last year, you're hiring an amateur. This isn't some unattainable goal or elite record-breaker status. Looking for an agent who is successful roughly once a week is eminently reasonable. Anything less and you're boarding an airplane with a rookie pilot.

A FULL-TIME AGENT

The real estate industry is full of part-timers, which is to say, amateurs. You wouldn't have surgery from a part-time doctor or hire a part-time lawyer, so why would you trust an asset worth hundreds of thousands of dollars to a part-timer? Make sure all agents you consider are full-time professionals who devote all their days to real estate, not the spare hours after they leave their other jobs.

We have shared with you so much in this book that it can become overwhelming. I hope that a lot of people will read this book and not do the same thing that has been done forever. They will hesitate calling the traditional agent they have always used. We need to stop thinking of house selling as a personal transaction. It's serious business and requires that you, as the seller, do your homework. As part of this, I definitely recommend that you at least interview a team of dynamic agents—such as our team—so you can see the difference.

SOCIAL MEDIA PRESENCE

You may think that focusing on social media is crazy, but in reality it is one of the most important pieces to the full-market-response puzzle. Social media is where everyone turns for the latest news, current events, updates on friends, and much more—so why not real estate? Life is now lived on devices. Therefore, social media has become the virtual stage where we are able to connect buyers and sellers. The agent that you hire should have a significant following on his or her business Facebook page. When I say significant, I mean twenty thousand-plus followers. The more activity the page has, the more traffic your home will receive. On the flip side, if you are a buyer, that significant following means access to additional potential sellers and more inventory for you to choose from. It's not just Facebook anymore either! You should be hiring an agent that is on Snapchat, Twitter, and Instagram. These are all marketing venues that ensure you are getting your home the maximum exposure and, in turn, maximizing your biggest investment. To be on the cutting edge of innovative advertising you need a dynamic agent who is constantly paying attention to upcoming platforms, testing them to see what works, and always looking for new ways to reach consumers.

CONTROL THE APPOINTMENT. ASK THE RIGHT QUESTIONS. MAKE MORE MONEY.

This is a very comprehensive list and can be overwhelming for most home sellers. We totally understand that! Realistically, the agent you are interviewing should be offering up this information at his or her presentation if that agent is selling services correctly. If an agent doesn't offer this information, here are the six most-vital questions you need to ask to make sure you are going to have a successful home sale. Remember, it's the process that puts more money in your pocket at the closing table—not the price.

1. Does the agent have a personal website that is not broker controlled? An agent needs this to be able to give your home the premarket promotion without accumulating any days on market.

2.   Are the agent's Zillow and Trulia profiles strong? How many sales and five-star reviews are on his or her profile? This is necessary so that when potential buyers view your home on these sites, they will contact the agent you selected to sell your home. If their profile is not strong, they will pick another agent who looks like the trusted local authority and who has most likely never been to your home.

3.   What is the agent's list-to-sales-price ratio? This is probably the most important question when comparing agents, as this tells you if he or she is able to sell homes for the price provided to clients, and it tells you if the agent is worth the commission he or she is asking. Finally, it helps you, the seller, know your bottom line, which is really the most important focus.

4.   What is the average number of days on the market for the agent's listings? This will help you know how quickly you can expect your home to sell and how many additional expenses you may have in carrying costs.

5.   What kind of marketing budget and marketing plan will the agent be using? If an agent is only selling four homes a year, he or she is not going to be able to use as much commission toward marketing, as the budget simply isn't there.

6.   Does the agent have a large enough database? To get you a full-market response, an agent needs to be able to reach out to thousands upon thousands of potential buyers, other real estate agents, and your community.

CONCLUSION

EMPOWERING YOU TO CHOOSE THE RIGHT TEAM

elling your home presents a unique set of challenges. It's probably your biggest asset, which means that choosing the right real estate agent and strategy is one of the most important business decisions of your life. At the same time, homeowners can feel quite emotional about this asset and make decisions with heads less clear than they should be. If they haven't read this book, for instance, most sellers don't know the difference between a traditional agent using a dated process and a dynamic agent getting a full-market response.

I hope that after reading this book, you now understand how important the difference is and realize that the traditional approach to selling your home can cost you significant amounts of time and money. It's not surprising that most consumers don't know that there's a much more effective alternative to the traditional approach, since most real estate agents don't know this either. They're doing the best they can, but they never get beyond the day-to-day struggle to find a few listings and put food on the table. It took me thousands of sales and years of experience to perfect the innovative marketing strategy that gets my sellers the full-market response their homes deserve.

My greatest reward in writing this book is knowing that I've debunked the many myths the traditional home-selling process relies on and armed you with the tools to hire a real estate team that can boost your bottom line in any market or location. I hope that you're now feeling empowered by knowing the difference between the traditional practices still standard in the industry and a newer, more-effective way to sell your property. My goal is that when you finally fold your arms and say "SOLD!" it will be with a smile, knowing you truly got the most the market would bear for your home, in the shortest time possible.

Knowledge is power, but knowledge without action is meaningless. My only request is that you promise to take your due diligence seriously when you hire a real estate agent. You now know that the traditional list-and-pray approach is not good enough, and you know all the right questions to ask in order to find someone who can deliver a better, proven process. Use the checklist I provided in chapter 12 to make sure that every aspect of your home sale gets the attention it warrants. Make sure that you have a professional team in your corner.

I provided a lot of information about the nuts and bolts of the sales process and what agents are doing—or not doing—behind the scenes to impress on you that a traditional agent working alone, or perhaps with one assistant, does not have the resources to do a good job, no matter how good his or her intentions. You will need expert advice on staging, understanding your buyers' psychology, making necessary improvements, getting premier architectural photography, pricing correctly, negotiating strategically, marketing creatively . . .

the list goes on. In fact, if I had to do all the necessary tasks on my own, I'd be overwhelmed. That's why I depend on my team of specialists and why my team is so successful.

Using the exclusive marketing system outlined in this book, my team and I continue to grow at an astronomical rate. We're doing our part to improve the industry by providing a level of customer service and a kind of full-market response unknown in the real estate industry until now. Educating you is part of that effort, and I hope this book helps you choose a team that makes you a winner at the closing table.

Thank you for reading, and a special thanks to our many clients and supporters. Without them, we never would have amassed the resources to create this state-of-the-art home-selling system or have been able to help so many sellers say, "SOLD!" with complete satisfaction.

krisl@krislindahl.com

763-244-2060

Official Partner of the
MINNESOTA WILD

Right: Kris Lindahl, Charlie Coyle, and Lindy. Far right: Linday. Below: Chris Hawkey from KFAN 100.3. Middle row, l-r: Aerial signage, billboard. Bottom row, l-r: Lindy at charity event; longest line of pumpkins; Kris with Guiness Book of World Records judge.

ABOUT MY TEAM

- Official Partner of The Minnesota Wild

- Exclusively endorsed by Chris Hawkey
  from KFAN 100.3

- Exclusively endorsed by Charlie Coyle
  from the Minnesota Wild

- Billboards throughout the metro area

- Aerial advertising with our plane

- Actively involved in community and local charities

- Guinness World Record holder (longest line of pumpkins)

- Furry, loveable mascot to make our
  experience better for all ages

WEBSITES

KrisLindahl.com   MinneapolisRealEstate.com

SaintPaulRealEstate.com   DuluthRealEstate.com

RochesterRealEstate.com   NewConstruction.com

 FB.com/KrisLindahlRealEstate

 https://www.snapchat.com/add/krislindahl

 http://www.zillow.com/profile/Kris-Lindahl/

 http://App.KrisLindahl.com

ABOUT THE AUTHOR

From an early age Kris recognized an internal need to make an impact on the world—*leave a legacy*. This drive and vision didn't include having one of the most successful real estate teams in the country, but that is the vehicle he created to turn that dream into a reality. His passion for teaching and inspiring those around him is contagious. Kris has taken the appetite for helping everyone and made it relevant to the real estate industry through serving his team and his community.

The Kris Lindahl Team is based on core values and a mission statement that was derived directly from his desire to provide positive influence in every aspect of his life. He and his team of real estate rock stars take pride in ensuring each client experience is amazing, every piece of marketing is innovative, and there is never a dollar left on the closing table that should have been in the client's pocket. In addition to their clients, they also strive to aid the neighborhood they call home through supporting schools, allocating generous funds to charities, and giving back with free events the entire family can enjoy.

The devotion that Kris and his team have to his mission is unsurpassed. Their authentic kindness, undying positivity, giving spirit, and perseverance to continuously provide has no other motive than to leave the world a better place than they found it. *This is his legacy.*

CPSIA information can be obtained
at www.ICGtesting.com
Printed in the USA
FSOW03n1938090117
29434FS